I0841497

"CLOSE TO YOU"

"WHY DO BIRDS SUDDENLY APPEAR

EVERY TIME YOU ARE NEAR?

JUST LIKE ME

THEY LONG TO BE CLOSE TO YOU

WHY DO STARS FALL DOWN FROM THE SKY

EVERY TIME YOU WALK BY?

JUST LIKE ME

THEY LONG TO BE

CLOSE TO YOU

THAT IS WHY ALL THE GUYS IN TOWN

FOLLOW YOU ALL AROUND

JUST LIKE ME

THEY LONG TO BE

CLOSE TO YOU"

"RON ISLEY & LAURYN HILL VERSION"

This is an inspirational story about how a loving relationship is a beautiful thing. When self-sacrifice and a giving attitude are displayed by both sides when realize that it's a marathon and not a sprint.

This story also gives the side of what happens when you are not willing to put the work in and leave the relationship for personal gain.

"Love conquers all in this story of my three sons. For couples so eager to call it quits after the infatuation wears off, to throw in the towel on your relationship because everything isn't 'perfect'. Lifelong commitment is not what most people think it is. It's not waking up every morning to make breakfast and eat together. It's not cuddling in bed until both of you fall asleep. It's not a clean home, filled with laughter and lovemaking every day. It's someone who steals all the covers, and snores, it's slammed doors and a few harsh words at times. It's stubbornly disagreeing and giving each other the silent treatment until your hearts heal, and then offering forgiveness. It's coming home to the same person every day that you know loves and cares about you in spite of, and because of, who you are. It's laughing about the one time you accidentally did something stupid. It's about dirty laundry and unmade beds. It's about

helping each other with the hard work of life. It's about swallowing the nagging words instead of saying them out loud. It's about eating the easiest meal you can make and sitting down together at a late hour because you both had a crazy day. It's when you have an emotional breakdown and your love lays down with you and holds you, and tells you everything is going to be okay. And you believe them. It's about still loving someone even though sometimes they make you absolutely insane. Loving someone isn't always easy, sometimes it's hard. But it is amazing and comforting and one of the best things you will ever experience."

STATEMENT BY

"VICTOR FORTENBERRY"

PREFACE

I loved Nancy. We dated for years, but she didn't know it. I first laid eyes on her when she was waiting at the bus stop with her younger brother. She was in the eleventh grade, and I was in the fifth grade. He was in my class. When he got on the bus, I slid over so he could sit down. I gave him a pound and said, "Man, your mama is fine." I saw movement from the corner of my eye. It was Nancy she placed her hand against the window I immediately put my hand against hers, and our relationship was consummated. He said, "Nancy is not my mother, she is my sister." From that day forward, I went over to his house every day after school just to be close to Nancy. But she was never home. I made sure we locked eyes and waved at each other every morning as the bus drove away.

I received bad news that Nancy had a new boyfriend and moved away. A part of me died that day. I continued to follow Nancy's life through her best friend, Sheila. Sheila was fine, too, but she was no Nancy Hussle.

My name is Nancy Hussle. I come from a two-parent home; my mother is named Katheryn, and her friends call her Kat. My father is Jerome Hussle, and his friends call him Rome. Both of my parents have decent jobs. My mother is a paralegal, and my father is a garbage man. I have three siblings, one older and two younger brothers. My oldest brother came from my father's first wife. We were all born and raised in Oakland, California. We lived a half mile from Knowland Park Zoo. My youngest brother and I attended Catholic school. We went to St. Louis Bertrand from first grade through eighth grade. From the ninth grade to the twelfth, we attended Bishop O. Dowd High School. My oldest brother and the brother under me went to public schools, King Jr. High, and Castlemont High School. Those two brothers fought anyone, anywhere, at any time. There was not a day that I can remember they didn't come home bleeding or with torn clothes. My parents had great hopes for me. But I couldn't leave the hood brothers alone.

Through high school, I was an all-A student. I learned and spoke three languages fluently. I played on the basketball team, baseball team, and ran track. My future was bright, and I received letters from several prestigious colleges, but my mind was still on having fun.

On Wednesday nights, I was at the San Leandro Skating Ring and the MOJO Skating Ring in East Oakland on Friday nights. Me and my girls drove the fellas crazy. Hanging out at Lake Merritt on Sundays after church, sitting in the fly rides of the Doe boys, was what we did. Going to college could wait.

I come off as nice and sweet until you try me. I learned from my brothers that the fight could be over while we were going in circles waiting for the first punch to be thrown. So, I would take the first swing. Oh, I have that fire in me! Don't let the small waist and cute face fool you. I stand 5'8 and weigh 155 pounds. When I extend my left arm, measure you for distance, and point my finger, my right hand is coming baby. I was a tomboy growing up - dirt bikes, scooters, and motorcycles. I fish and hunt.

My father spent a lot of time nurturing my older brother into a man, teaching him how to do all the things he couldn't afford to do growing up. Because I was right behind my brother in age, my father gladly brought me up the same way. As a female, I loved being part of the 4H Club. We made up new dances every week and volunteered in the community.

At eighteen, I met a guy named Destin Balin at the San Leandro Skating Ring on a Wednesday night. He was an older man, twenty-five years old, with his own place. I believed every word he fed me. I was ready to leave home and he wanted me to move in. I got a job in the San Leandro Shopping Mall at Bay Fair Center, and we were a happy couple.

I must admit I was a jealous woman. I had a good-looking man and didn't want any woman next to him but me. I stepped in between him and his mama if they hugged too long.

Destin graduated from Castlemont High School. He was a smart brother who always kept a job. Destin worked two jobs when I first moved in with him. When I began working, he found a better-paying job at a shoe store in San Leandro. This allowed him to quit the other two jobs and us to ride to work and home together.

When you live with someone for a while, you realize that their game is not as tight as they make it out to be. We were not advancing in life, and I had too many men telling me I was a queen, royalty, and born to be respected. But I didn't feel like it. I knew Destin didn't sell dope, but one day, I encouraged him to at least try it for a while. We were poor in my book, and I could hear my father's voice saying, "You could do bad by yourself." My mother would always say, "I said a prayer for you."

PUBLISHER'S NOTE:

This is a work of fiction. Names, characters, places, and incidents either are the product of the author's imagination or are used fictitiously, and any resemblance to actual persons living or dead, events, or locales is entirely coincidental.

TABLE OF CONTENTS

MY III SONS

CHAPTER 1

SAY A LITTLE PRAYER FOR YOU

This story began with a young man named Destin Balin, who lived with his girlfriend, Nancy Hussle, and their son, DJ (Destin Junior), in Oakland, California. They struggled as a family but enjoyed parks, beaches, skating rings, movies, rap concerts, and birthday parties. When times were good, they took a trip to Las Vegas. This was within their budget. Once DJ was born, everything changed. Nancy gave Destin a child because he promised her the world when they first met and didn't deliver on any promises except for knocking her up and producing a beautiful son. Nancy dreamed big and wanted a house, a nice car, and a life she thought she deserved. Destin had several ideas that would bring in more money, but that meant being away from home, and Nancy wasn't having it.

One afternoon, Destin contacted Nancy and asked her to get dressed up because he had a surprise and wanted to celebrate. Nancy put on her silk black dress with the spaghetti straps, and the back out, finishing the look with black, five-inch pumps with gold heels. She was expecting to hear Destin had received a promotion that would get them up, and out of the hood. Or, had a new job paying more money that would get them up, and out of the hood. Nancy rehearsed her reactions in the mirror several times. She screamed with excitement, some in shock, covering her mouth, speechless, and with teary eyes.

On the way to pick up Nancy, Destin began rehearsing his proposal. Most of it sounded like a long, boring speech that he didn't even like. By the time he got home, Destin decided to go with the flow of the night. Nancy was waiting at the door and wrapped her arms around Destin's neck as soon as he walked over the threshold. She delivered a big juicy kiss on him and asked, "What's the surprise?" Destin, going with the flow of the evening, fell on one knee. Nancy stared down at him, raised her dress, and said, "Is this what you want?"

Destin began to pat his pockets in search of the ring and whipped out a small black box while smiling like the Grinch who stole Christmas. Nancy pulled the .45-carat diamond ring out of the box and said, "Oh, hell no!" She placed it back into the box and closed the top. Destin stood up to see Nancy's index finger just centimeters from his nose. She shouted, "This ring won't get us out of here. I'd rather you used that money to move us into a better neighborhood." The two of them heatedly argued, and Nancy decided to leave and take their son, DJ, with her. Destin was willing to fight to keep DJ; he loved his son like nothing else in the world. She knew this and said, "DJ can live with you until I graduate with my master's degree and get things set up to take care of my son." Destin agreed, knowing it would be years before Nancy could pull this off.

When Nancy closed the door, with all of her belongings removed from the apartment and packed into her little Toyota Corolla, Destin began doing the "Running Man" and then the "Dougie" until he looked over at DJ standing in front of the window crying as his mother drove away. He watched as DJ mouthed the words "say a little prayer for you" to her. Destin celebrated only because Nancy was putting demands on him and not allowing him to fulfill them. "Put us first. You need to bring in more money. When are we going to move? I want a new car." Nancy had Destin by the balls. When she walked out that door, a weight lifted off Destin, and he began to dance.

DJ hated this arrangement and cried every night for months. As a child, he was an emotional wreck. DJ learned how to tell time early in life because he knew his mother would call every morning at 8:00

a.m. before he left for school. He loved to hear the sound of his mother's voice. DJ knew the morning conversations would be short, so he listened as Nancy prayed for him. Their Saturday conversations were longer. DJ would rise early, parading around with his Spiderman pajamas on, turn on Saturday morning cartoons, and eat a bowl of cereal in front of the television until his mother called.

DJ had trouble sleeping at night when Nancy first left the home, so Destin would put wine in his Kool-Aid to help him sleep. The problem with doing that was it caused DJ to sleep hard, and he would wet the bed. Destin learned a lot about himself and raising a child alone.

Destin didn't make a lot of money at his job selling shoes. He made enough to keep a roof over their heads and food on the table. As DJ grew older, Destin signed him up for sports, and when he wasn't practicing or playing in a game, he was riding his bike. DJ ruled the world when he was riding and would be gone for hours. He found a dirt bike racing facility in Brookfield Village and would spend the day watching races from outside the fence, dreaming of the day he would race and beat them all. One afternoon, DJ arrived home after watching a kid from his school race and told his father about it. They went and watched bike races all day. Now he had to figure out how to raise enough money to get DJ in a race.

Destin had a buddy named Robby, who worked at the radio station *KNOD* in Oakland. Robby worked the night shift but was studying to be an engineer; he could create beats to enhance any song. One night, Robby called Destin and told him he had two tickets to one of the biggest Rap concerts of their time. Before Destin knew the date, he agreed to go. The concert was two weeks away, and he lined up a babysitter to stay with DJ for the night.

Seven of the top rappers performed, and the headliner was The Dream. The Dream was the man; his raps excited and motivated you! The concert lasted for eight hours. Destin came home inspired and made up his mind that he would become a rapper at the age of thirty-two.

Destin fell into a deep sleep, tired from the eight-hour concert. He slept most of the next day and awoke to a strained voice from yelling out the rap songs' lyrics. DJ stayed two apartment units down and was outside playing with friends when Destin heard his voice and went outside. DJ saw him and gave Destin a big hug.

They lived in a two-bedroom apartment on the east side of Oakland, off 90th Avenue. Destin dropped DJ off every day for school, then drove to San Leandro to work at Burks Shoe Store. Burks carried mostly women's shoes and a small selection for men. There were very few customers in the morning until the lunch crowd came through. People would stop by the small shoe store in the strip mall after eating next door at Fong's Chinese Restaurant. This gave Destin time to work on his rap lyrics. He had a tablet and pen by his side at all times and would write his rhymes throughout the day.

After two weeks of writing, starting over, and rewriting, Destin came up with what he thought was a masterpiece. After work, he drove over to Robby's house and showed him the lyrics. He laughed, "Oh, you gon' be a wack rapper? There's a reason you sell shoes for a living." He could see where Destin was going with his concept but needed to hear it out loud.

"Destin, my man, it's hard out here. Carry this gun.

I ain't about that life. I love my girl and my son.

Life is short. I'm not running with the big dawgs. I'm a stay on the porch.

I'm going to be the best rapper. I'm going to church. I'm not about that life. I believe in family first.

I'm going to keep it real. I have to work. What will my son do without me if I'm lying dead in the dirt?

My life is going somewhere. I'm not your average rapper, I don't care if you stare. I pull my pants up. I don't have braids; I brush my hair.

I don't wear any gold. I put that money away for when I get old."

Robby lived in a house left to him by his grandmother. One of the rooms in the house was converted into a sound booth. He had Destin go inside and read his lyrics. They both agreed it didn't sound as good as it did on paper. Robby said, "Let me work my magic. We may have to do a couple of more sessions in the booth, but I think I can turn this into something." Destin left Robby's house excited because he knew Robby was going to become a great engineer and producer. He was talented in that way.

Two days later, Robby called Destin and asked him to stop by his house to listen to his hot new rap song. Destin almost passed out once he heard his voice with the music.

Destin asked, "What's next?"

"I will take it to work and try it out on my session called 'Love it or Dump it'. If it does well, I will ask one of the daytime DJs to play it and get listener feedback", Robby replied.

Destin was reciting the lyrics to his song all day at work and all evening at home. He played it for DJ who recognized his voice immediately and began dancing to the beat. DJ memorized the lyrics, and they had rap battles with the one song. Destin wanted to get DJ into a better school and better neighborhood, and this might be his chance.

Robby called Destin and told him the song did well on his midnight show. He would leave it for one of his co-workers to play on the morning show. The school kids and morning commuters would be their target.

The song was played every hour. It was the most requested song of the day. Robby called Destin and asked him to stop by the radio station when he got off work. He showed up at *KNOD* at about 7 p.m. Robby was waiting on him and they walked into a conference room where two men and a woman were sitting and conversing. The producers looked at Destin through the window and were shocked by his appearance. He wore a shirt and tie with Dickie pants and Penny Loafers. No dreadlocks, no gold in his mouth. He even wore a part in his hair. His background check showed he has never had a parking ticket. They wondered if he spoke well. "Who's going to follow such a clean-cut rapper?"

Robby introduced them as the CEOs of Track Sound Music, the hottest new record label. "Mr. Destin Balin, we would like to offer you a record deal and sign you to our label. In this deal, we offer you $10,000. We have several commercials and movies that would like to use your rap song. Royalties will also be paid to you on any deal where your song is played. We need to set up a tour date to get your name and face out there if you accept."

Destin beamed, "I accept."

The deal was done.

"Robby will be your DJ, if that's okay with you? What do you call yourself?"

"DJB!"

"You are now DJB and Robby Rock," said one of the CEOs.

"Robby, you have a contract too?" added Destin.

"Yep, you eat, we eat. Let's make this money."

Destin was a 32-year-old, 6'3", clean-cut father of one. He planned to invest his money because he didn't know how long this ride would last. He and Robby grew up together and played on the same basketball team through high school. They went their separate ways when Destin became a father and settled down with Nancy.

The song became a bigger hit than anyone could expect. It was the most requested song across the country and held the #1 slot in the ratings for months; a one-hit wonder. Track Sound Music kept Destin hidden until the tour for two reasons. He only had a single for one, and he didn't have an image for two. The music video would expose him and the label wasn't ready for that.

In the meantime, Destin moved to the Oakland Hills and rented an affordable three-bedroom, two-bathroom house for himself and DJ. He looked into renting a condo, but DJ would have to carry his bike up and down the stairs every day. Neighbors were on both sides of him and across the street. Destin wanted to be able to make noise and have friends over without anyone complaining. DJ had a few problems with the new living arrangements, also. There were no corner stores, too many hills, and he didn't know anyone in the neighborhood. Destin fixed that immediately. He bought DJ a moped. DJ was 11 years old and never dreamed of owning a moped at that age. Destin explained to him that if the moped got him into trouble or his grades drop, he would take it away.

CHAPTER 2

MY BROTHER FOR LIFE

DJ was riding through the neighborhood when he recognized a fat kid from school. "What was he doing up here?" DJ thought. They began talking, and DJ found out his name was Fitzgerald. His nickname Fatz. Understandably so. Like DJ, Fatz's mom got a better job and moved them out of the old neighborhood and into the Hills where Fatz could receive a better education. Fatz was 15 years old, 6 feet, and 220 pounds. Solid. They began hanging out every day after school and on the weekends.

He brought Fatz home one day because Destin wanted to meet whom he was hanging out with every day. They walked in, and Destin and Robby were working on his next single. Fatz walked up to Destin, "My name is Fatz. I know who you are by your voice. My mom plays your song in the car all the time."

"Glad to meet you Fatz."

"It's Fitzgerald, but everyone calls me Fatz."

"Ok, Fatz, this is DJ Robby Rock."

"DJ Robby Rock from *KNOD*, the late-night mixer?"

"In the flesh. A pleasure to meet you Fatz."

Fatz was over at DJ's house every day after school. He had no brothers or sisters and spent a lot of time alone once he and his mom moved into the Oakland Hills. Faye, Fatz's mother, worked for a marketing company right out of high school. She began college at USC in Los Angeles but got sidetracked. Pregnant with Fatz her sophomore year, she moved back home. Faye works during the day and takes classes at Chabot Community College at night. She does the best she can as a single mother. Fatz is a good kid and stays out of trouble, but her biggest fear is that it won't last long.

Faye heard the name DJ every day. That's all Fatz talks about. After night school, every evening, she picked him up from DJ's house. One evening Faye decides to get out of the car and ring the doorbell. To her surprise, a very good-looking, tall, masculine man with a pleasant smile answered the door, "You must be Fatz's mom. Come on in." Faye walked into a clean, well-furnished home with beautiful artwork and attractively colored accessories. "Please have a seat," Destin said.

"The boys are in the backroom playing video games. Would you like something to eat or drink?"

"Eat? Yes. Fatz cooked tonight. I told him if he's going to be hanging out around here, he's going to have to help out. Thursday nights he cooks. Fatz does love to cook. I would like to take this time to thank you for allowing my son into your home. You have been a blessing to me more than you will ever know. If I can return the favor just ask. I will make it happen."

Faye winked at Destin, and the deal was done. They began a relationship, but the boys never knew.

Fatz became like a second son to Destin, and on his birthday, he bought Fatz a moped. DJ and Fatz took off and didn't come back until the early morning hours. Faye and Destin took this time to bump and grind at his house because previously, they went to Faye's condo while the boys were at his house.

Summer arrived, and Destin began his first tour. He was the opening act because he had only two songs for now. Destin didn't mind; there was no way he wanted to go on after some of these gold and platinum album rappers. He requested two stools placed on stage for DJ and Fatz. Stage time was approximately fifteen minutes, and Destin didn't have to work hard because the crowd rapped the entire song with him. At times, he held the mic out toward the crowd and let them recite the lyrics. Robby would remix the song into a version they never heard, and they sang it again.

DJ would be on his feet, dancing and saying the lyrics with the fans. He was Destin's hype man. Fatz sat on his bar stool, eating the whole fifteen minutes; usually, hamburgers, fries, and a chocolate shake. Destin and Robby earned $15,000 each for a show. Not bad for fifteen minutes. Once they cut more songs, they would get more time and receive bigger checks. But for now, they were both happy with the income.

All summer long this was the routine. Destin's face was out there, he wore blue jeans a sweatshirt, and tennis shoes. No gold, no braids, no dancers, except for DJ. And no entourage. He met all the big-name rappers on the tour. Some rappers would leave touring due to court dates, baby mama drama, entourage disputes, and payment problems for showing up late. Destin was the oldest rapper on the tour and carried himself more like an uncle to everyone. He had a lot of sit-down talks with the rappers on conducting business as a young man.

Destin never messed around with the women that were allowed backstage. He made sure DJ and Fatz stayed away from the rappers when they were getting high. He took good care of his kids and made sure their school work was completed when he traveled during the school year.

Network television noticed Destin's story in the tabloids and offered him a reality show. They thought the way he carried himself in public, and the care of his two children was an amazing thing to see a rapper do. Destin signed a $1 million deal for one season with thirteen episodes. The checks would be larger if the show was picked up for more seasons.

The owner of the house Destin was renting found out movie cameras, and people were in and out of their house all day and night and immediately raised the rent. He paid it because there were two months left on his rental contract. The network found Destin a home, but he had to move to Los Angeles. Destin knew this was a game-changer for him and DJ. He sat down with Faye and Fatz to discuss his plans going forward. He offered to take Fatz with him and continue to co-raise him. Faye could come and stay whenever she pleased. To Destin's surprise, Faye agreed wholeheartedly. Fay trusted Destin and believed that he represented how a man should provide and be a leader in the household.

CHAPTER 3

LIVING LIFE IN THE LIMELIGHT

Two weeks later, they had moved to Los Angeles into a 4,500-square-foothome in the valley. DJ, now 14 years old, breathed motocross bike racing. Fatz, now 17 years old, played football in high school in the linebacker position. He is putting players to sleep on the field. His natural size and increased muscle made him a pure beast. The reality show loved the idea because this would give them more to film and see how Destin juggled all the parenting issues as a single father. Every Saturday morning, they traveled to a new city for DJ to compete after watching Fatz play Friday night under the lights.

Destin didn't have time to write another rap song with all the different activities going on. But DJ did. DJ would write when he was out with his new motocross buddies. All of them were from wealthy families, some white, some black, and some Asian. All they cared about was riding hard in the dirt and jumping over obstacles. That's what DJ wrote about. He rapped it in his mind and shared it with the fellas. They critiqued it, and DJ made changes here and there until he had a solid twelve songs.

Twice a week Destin required the boys to put aside whatever they were doing to have family time together. They enjoyed this time together because both of them were coming into their own.

Fatz had a couple of girlfriends now, and Destin constantly stayed on him about how to treat them, and how hard it would be if he had to take care of a baby. Fatz thought about his life coming up and understood what Destin told him. Fatz had grown to be a very handsome young man, mild-mannered with soft eyes that drove the girls crazy. Fatz was sexing the ladies down one after another. He also spent time with the chef hired by the network to cook for the family and learned some cooking secrets. Fatz and Chef Royal created recipes right there during the reality show. Royal would have him research ingredients and explain to the viewers the origin of the plant or seasoning, where it could be found in stores, and also discuss the flavor of the food. The first bite should explode with flavor in your mouth, savor the taste, and try to figure out what flavor you're tasting. Chef Royal discussed which wines paired best with certain meals. Fatz did his research daily and became articulate in culinary language. Over two million viewers watched every show! Unknowingly, Fatz created a fan base that launched talks with the network to create a spinoff reality show called *Fatz Cuisine*.

DJ handed over his greatest hits to his father. Destin asked, "What is this?"

"This is a sample of my greatest hits. I need Robby to produce a beat for them."

"Son, are you serious? I didn't know you wanted to rap."

They all sat there with smiles on their faces.

"Pop, I enjoyed the energy of the crowd when you performed. That's why I always got up and danced. If you were on the stage for only fifteen minutes and made $15,000, I figure I could bring in at least $50,000 a show.

"Well, it's time for me to share what I've been doing. I wrote another rap song and Robby is producing the music for it. We can go on tour together now that we both will be rappers."

On DJ's way home from a long afternoon of motocross riding, he turned on his street and saw a small child wearing a t-shirt and the Hulk shorts. With a camera crew in tow, he stopped to see who this child was and why he was outside alone. (The camera crew followed DJ everywhere he went.)

DJ asked the little boy, who looked to be about 3 or 4 years old, "Where do you live?" The little boy pointed in two different directions. "Where's your mother?" The little boy hunched his shoulders. DJ told the camera crew he was taking the little boy home to his father because he didn't want to leave him outside in the hot sun. The camera crew agreed.

"Hey Pop, are you home? I have a gift for you." Destin ran out of his room and said, "I love gifts. I'm coming. A baby? Really!"

"He was out in the middle of the street when I rode up the block. I couldn't leave him out there."

"Ok, you did the right thing. But why does he stink?"

"I was thinking the same thing."

"What's his name?"

"I don't know, but right now, I'm going to call him Booboo.

"I will take him, get him cleaned up, and we will go to find his parents." Destin frowned as he walked with the little boy to the bathroom. He stripped the boy's clothes off and put him in the shower. He dug out some of DJ's old clothes and tried to make them fit just long enough to get the boy home.

Destin, DJ, Booboo, and the camera crew left the house to find his parents. It didn't take long; a lady stood in the middle of the street where DJ found the little boy looking distressed. When she saw them coming her way, she cried, "That's my baby!" Destin asked her if she was okay.

"Why?" was her response.

"Because you look a hot mess."

"Look at your son. He's all dusty and dirty. He looks a hot mess." DJ stood there full of dirt from head to toe.

"Take your son. We cleaned up Booboo."

"Why are you calling him Booboo? His name is Raphael."

"He messed himself and smelled like Booboo, so we called him Booboo. My name is Destin and this is my son DJ."

"I'm Grace, thank you for bringing my son back to me."

Destin thought she was a good-looking woman, with beautiful features, caramel-colored skin, nice teeth, and soft brown eyes. But Grace looked like she had been smoking crack or meth or something. Her eyes were red from crying. She took Raphael by the hand and walked him home, six houses down the street.

CHAPTER 4

THIS IS GAME MAMA

Fatz received offers from twelve colleges to play football. Destin told him that he had a decision to make. "Your mom is coming here to see you tomorrow, and we also need to discuss what you are going to do about your cooking show. The networks have been hounding me about it." Said, Destin.

"They reached out to me also. Here's the money they're offering per season. I told them I had to run it by you first."

"Thank you Fatz. We need to agree on this as a family. Wow! That's a lot of money."

"I know. I was nervous just looking at all of those zeros."

Faye arrived safely, and everyone was happy to see her. Fatz hugged his mom while smiling, "Hey, Mama."

"Hi, baby. Hello Destin! Oh, what a nice hug. Hello DJ. Wow, you're getting tall. Destin, you said we have some family business to discuss."

"Yes, Fatz has several colleges submitting offers and a reality show offer that we need to address.

"You're the man of the house. I'm listening."

"Fatz has to make up his mind about what school he wants to attend. He's leaning toward USC. Because Fatz is already part of our *Destin Family Reality Show*, as a fan favorite, the network will increase his offer as time goes on as long as he continues to have a following. Fatz, show your mom the offer." He pulled out the offer letter and laid it on the table. Faye cleared her throat, "Are you kidding me? All of this for one season. For a cooking show? Here I am. I just completed my Master's and received an offer from a marketing company for $150,000 a year, and you've been offered a couple of million for a cooking show?" Faye fanned herself with the paper from Fatz.

"It's not your fault, Mom. The government tricked millions of people into going to college. I hate that you went through this, but it was a way to keep our people from receiving good jobs. Whenever we figure out a way to keep up, they come up with something else. Luckily for me, I've come up during a time when I can make millions on the internet and never work a nine to five.

"I have $100,000 in school loans that I owe. This is amazing. I remember when they wouldn't give you a decent-paying job without a college degree. I worked my butt off competing for jobs to survive in this world." Fatz pulled out another sheet of paper and handed it to his mom. "What's this son?"

"My bank statements."

"How do you have this much money in the bank with no job?"

"My job is a reality show. I have 15 million followers."

Destin explained, "Fatz is a big part of the show. He's funny and tells stories while cooking. He has lots of secret ingredients and people tune in to see what he's cooking."

"Destin you pay my son that much money, and now he has an offer for his very own show?" Tears welled up in her eyes. "Mama, I'm going to write you a check to pay off your student loans." He immediately looked over at Destin as if to get approval, and Destin nodded his head.

Faye asked Destin if she could speak to him in private. Faye hugged the boys again, and they went to Destin's bedroom for two hours. Nothing but bumping and grinding. Faye reminded Destin of Jill Scott; he loved her smile and attitude. Her drive to accomplish goals was unmatched. Destin asked Faye to move in, but she declined, stating the time was not right and she couldn't do this Hollywood stuff. "I can't live with people in my business 24/7." Destin understood. He pulled the covers over them and went back to pushing and shoving.

CHAPTER 5

LITTLE MAN IS BACK

DJ pulled up to the house on his motorcycle and saw Booboo sitting on the curb in front of his house. Booboo heard and saw him coming and stood up, raising his hands as if he were happy to see him. DJ got off his bike to talk to Booboo. Again, he was smelly and needed a shower. DJ held his hand, walked him into the house, and started the shower. Thank God he was only flatulent, and there was no mess to clean up.

One hour later, Grace showed up at the door looking bad. Destin invited her in and stood in front of her shaking his head. He asked, "Can I offer you something to drink?"

"No, I won't be here that long. I came to pick up Raphael, and we're going home.

"I can tell you're a private person, but I would like to help you get through whatever this is you're doing.

"No, I don't need any help. Raphael sneaks out while I'm napping."

"When you want to nap, send him down here so he doesn't have to sneak out. We will watch him."

Grace broke down and told Destin she married a baseball player she met in college. "He was Dominican, very handsome, and smart. I was studying to be a Chemist. Believe it or not, I'm intelligent. Once he signed with the Dodgers things changed. We were invited to parties once a week. I got hooked on cocaine. He wouldn't touch the stuff because of drug testing in the MLB organization. After Raphael was born, he began leaving me home in his off-season. He bought this house years ago and has never been here longer than a month."

"I understand. If you will allow me to help you, I will keep Raphael here safe in my home while you attend a drug treatment program. Is that a deal we can make? It's a year-long program and you have to complete it."

"Why do you want to help me? You don't know me nor do you owe me anything."

"Fatz is not my child but I raise him as if he were. I'm willing to do the same for you and your son. Yes, or no? I'm not asking again."

Grace nodded in agreement, fell into Destin's arms, and sobbed uncontrollably until she was sick. Snot and slob decorated his shirt. He looked down at her and pressed her head closer to his chest.

Fatz was at USC breaking guys in half and folding them over like paper. He averaged nine tackles a game. At the middle linebacker position, he forced the offense to run their plays to the opposite side of the field. His speed was unmatched by anyone else playing this position. He was a beast. Some seniors were not happy with the decision to nominate Fatz as defense captain as a freshman after the third week of play. But after witnessing his leadership and play on the field, all accepted and respected him. It was a known fact that as a 19-year-old, he bench-pressed close to 500 pounds and squatted 600 pounds. Fatz stood 6'4" and weighed 275 pounds. He would likely leave college early and enter the draft. Right now, he looked like a number one draft pick.

With all his success, Fatz always kept his reality show in the back of his head. Business management was his major, and Fatz excelled in all his classes, prioritizing football as secondary and his degree as primary. He was already a millionaire without signing a contract with any pro team. Fatz's business plan included owning a chain of fast-food restaurants, a five-star restaurant, and maybe a clothing store with sports apparel. Also, the World Wrestling Federation contacted him to make guest appearances.

Destin and DJ went home after a meeting with DJ Robby. He told them DJ's album would be platinum in a week. "I sampled some of the cuts and your fans are going wild. I get the midnight crowd. I can't wait to hear how all the early morning and lunchtime fans feel about you. I like that you're rapping about different things like the motocross life and the reality show life. Both of these things got you where you are today. You are hot right now."

"What about my single Robby, am I hot right now?" asked Destin.

"I haven't put music to yours, I've been working on DJ's. I will get you this week. I promise."

Grace had a difficult time adapting to her new environment. She went through withdrawals, and it took all the fight out of her. She was sick in the morning, at noon, and night. Grace would not eat, and when she did, she couldn't hold it down. They considered giving her drugs and weening her off of them. Nightly, Grace had an IV drip to keep fluids in her system. She had big dark circles around her eyes, barely weighed 100 pounds, and her hair began to fall out. Every day, she would injure herself, but not on purpose, it seemed to be accidental. For her safety, the facility staff placed Grace on suicide watch until her condition improved.

By the 90th day, Grace's appearance and demeanor had noticeably improved. She could have a conversation without crying or cursing out everyone. Her hair started to grow back; it had fallen out in so many places that they shaved her hair low.

No more deep, dark circles around her eyes displayed the beautiful brown eyes the staff adored. Grace now received her property to keep in her room. They delivered all eight of her study books from college. She thought while she was in rehab cleaning up her act, she would refresh her knowledge and prepare to enter the working world.

Dream, the best rapper in the game, made an appointment to meet with Destin. "My brother, it's been a while since we've talked. Is everything good?" he asked.

"Living the dream. I wanted to meet with you because I heard your son's soundtrack, and I loved it."

"How did you hear his soundtrack? We just heard it two days ago."

"Come on now, Destin, I'm Dream. Nothing in the music industry gets past me. Plus, I'm a fan of the show, and I move how you move. Just like that. I have a question for you. I know you're working on another hit, and with your son's dope album about to drop, I want you guys to come on tour with me. We're taking it internationally."

"Please tell me you're bullshitting. DJ loves you. He is going to lose his mind when he hears this."

"Is he around? The last time I saw him he was sitting on the stool on stage while you were performing. Then he would get up and dance and drive the crowd crazy. Your little man has talent. Speaking of talent where is Fatz? I went to a USC home game and that boy is scary to watch. I can't imagine what it feels like to receive one of his hits. Someone gets carried off the field every game."

"He is truly Boyz II Men. A gentle person that loves his family."

DJ walked in the back door from taking Booboo for a ride on his motorcycle. He saw Dream, ran to him, and hugged him tight around the waist. Booboo, not far behind, did the same thing. Dream hugged DJ back, picked up Booboo, and asked, "Who is this little man?"

Destin nodded in his son's direction. "Tell him Dream."

"My man, I want you and your father to go on tour with me." DJ looked at his father, then back at Dream with big crocodile tears welling up in his eyes that rolled down his face. Booboo looked at DJ sitting in the chair with his hands covering his face and started to cry with him. At six years old, Booboo did whatever DJ did. They are as close as father and son.

"I guess that's a yes, says Dream. I'd like to seal this deal with a prayer if that's ok with you guys. A family that prays together stays together. I don't want any foolishness while we're overseas, that's why I'm coming to you with this offer. I like the way you conduct business, and everything you do seems to blossom. I have a lot of respect for you Destin. I've watched DJ grow up I see a lot of you in him. Who is this young man? What's his name? Raphael clings to him. That's love. My people will be in touch."

Destin, DJ, and Booboo did the happy dance. Whatever that is and whatever that looks like, they did it until they were satisfied.

CHAPTER 6

HOW QUICKLY THINGS CHANGE

Destin receives a phone call from Faye. "Hello, sweetheart. Do you miss me as much as I miss you? Come see big daddy."

"Destin, we need to talk. I met someone and I want to see if this is going somewhere. Before you get pissed off, I want to thank you for everything you have done for me and Fatz. I could have never raised Fatz into the man he has become. Because you came into his life, he now has opportunities that we could have never imagined. You are the most brilliant, dedicated, supportive, loving, and obedient man of God that I have ever met or will ever meet. I have no problem with you, and I will always love you. I pray that you understand and will remain close to me and my son for the rest of our lives. Please promise me that." What could Destin come back with after such a powerful, and meaningful monologue? He replied simply, "Okay!"

DJ Robby worked magic on Destin's rap song. Destin makes songs with easy lyrics to rap along to. Nothing hardcore. No cursing, and a lot of catchphrases. Grandmas love him because now they're in the game, quoting his lyrics to their grandkids. Robby calls and informs him that if he gets the same reaction as the last song he will be back on top. The record company created a category for his type of rap called "Easy Listening Rap. It spread like wildfire and all types of new rap artists were cutting singles.

The overseas tour began. Destin came out first and stretched two songs to twenty minutes, followed by DJ killing it for forty-five minutes. He came out to an instrumental beat of his number 1 hit, dressed in motocross gear down to the boots. DJ took center stage, removed his helmet, and Booboo jumped off the barstool to retrieve it. That was Booboo's contribution to the show. And Dream, the headliner, was on for as long as he felt like performing. Booboo had a seat on stage, with DJ by his side, when Destin performed. DJ had to get up and dance, and that's how he gained a lot of his followers. He had the most difficult dances on *TikTok*. There were constant hits on his page from all over the world of people trying to keep up with his steps.

As the tour continued, Dream noticed how the crowd reacted to DJ when he got up to dance to his father's rap. Dream offered DJ an additional $10,000 a show to dance before he took the stage. DJ refused the money and performed for free. The Dream wouldn't allow that and gave the money to Destin. He told Destin any time DJ was tired, he didn't have to go on for him. And what about Raphael? He did everything DJ did; Dream wanted him in on the act. The Dream turned on the music and said, "Let's see what you got, Raphael." After only thirty seconds, "I'm sorry, I can't use you."

DJ began posting videos of him teaching Raphael how to dance. The comments were brutal.

"Get that two left-footed fool out of here."

"He dances like Steve Martin in the movie, The Jerk."

"Is that child black? The rhythm left him."

These attacks went on until DJ decided to remove the videos. Raphael wasn't reading them, but this let him see how cruel the real world was. Destin began reading them and wanted to see how DJ handled it. He noticed that DJ never commented back. He removed the footage as if it never happened and kept on making videos.

Destin had a lot on his plate trying to keep up with all of the contracts, payroll, and taxes. He added and subtracted all day when they were not on tour. He felt like admitting himself into rehab just to rest. Destin figured Fatz's quarterly taxes because he wanted to know how much he owed before taking it to an accountant. He may not be exact, but he would come close. Destin learned this while working at the shoe store. "Don't despise these small beginnings, for the Lord rejoices to see the work begin." His mother always quoted that scripture when he complained about working at the shoe store and wanting to quit. Now Destin proclaimed, "Look at God!"

Destin used the calculator to add thousands of dollars and talked out loud as he keyed each amount. Booboo sat on the floor in the office and played with the toy motorcycles DJ bought for him. As Destin hit the equal key, Booboo said, "$678, 278.40." "How did you know that? You're seven years old", Destin blurted.

"I don't know. I heard you saying some numbers and I knew the answer."

"Did you just learn this?"

"Nope, you are the only person I've heard add up numbers out loud, but wherever I see numbers, I add them up."

"Subtraction too?"

"Sure!"

"Come here little man, I want you to look at something."

"My name is Booboo not little man."

Destin got a pillow, propped Booboo up in the chair and he went to work. He added, subtracted, multiplied, divided, and did percentages. Millions of dollars that took Destin sometimes two days were done in a half hour. Booboo climbed down out of the chair and started playing with his motorcycles again. Destin asked, "Is something wrong, why did you quit?"

"I didn't quit. I'm finished unless you have more you want me to do."

Destin fell to his knees next to Booboo and began bawling. He couldn't hold it back. Booboo patted him on his back, "It's okay. It's okay."

"Does your mother know you can do this?"

"I don't know."

"Can your mother do this?"

Booboo hunched his shoulders, "I don't know, ask her."

Destin called the rehab center to check on Grace's condition. They told him that she was doing fine and studying Biochemistry, so she could get back into the working world. Destin asked, "Can she have visitors?"

"Mr. Destin, Grace has two more months and her year is up. We would hate to see her decline because visitors do that to rehab patients. Can you hang on without her for two more months?"

"Absolutely!" Destin did the happy dance by himself. Booboo looked at him like he was tripping. How could he be on his knees crying one minute and dancing the next?

Booboo saw Fatz come through the door and ran to him. He started at his knee and climbed up this rock of a man. Fatz held him like a baby while Booboo wrapped his arms around his neck and squeezed tightly. He laid his head on Fatz's shoulder. His eyes started to water because he felt genuine love from the boy he considered his little brother. Booboo told him, "I love you and I missed you and I'm glad you're home." Fatz put him down, and Booboo tried to wrestle with him. Fatz picked him up by his ankle and walked around the house with him upside down trying to see where everyone else was. Booboo finally said, "Fatz, I'm getting dizzy."

"I'm sorry, Booboo. Let me put you down. I forgot how big this house was," Fatz apologized. From his bag, Fatz grabbed a football and a USC football helmet and gave them to Booboo. He ran outside and played catch by himself.

"Hey Dad, there you are."

"Hey son, I thought you were coming by later today. Are you staying with us?"

"Oh yeah, there's no place I'd rather be. Booboo stays here now?"

"Yes, until his mother, Grace, gets out of rehab next month. Come with me, I want to show you something. Booboo, come inside with me."

"What's going on Dad?"

"I want you to meet our new accountant."

"I don't get it. Help me understand."

"I was adding up your quarterly taxes on the calculator, but I was saying the numbers out loud.

Booboo heard me, added up the numbers in his head, and came up with the right amount. I let him complete your taxes, my taxes, and DJ's. He did it in thirty minutes."

"What do we do now?"

"I'm waiting for his mom to come home to find out how much she knows about his talent."

"Does DJ know?"

"No! I just found out this morning."

"Fatz, will you make me a Fatz Burger?" asked Booboo.

"Me too son, it has been a while since I've had one."

"I thought you all would never ask. Let me change my clothes."

The camera crew smelled the burgers, and without asking, Fatz whipped up several more. The doorbell rang, and it was the Dream.

""Hey everybody, hey Fatz. It's been a long time since I've seen you. I think it was at your father's concert. You were sitting on a stool during the show eating a burger and fries. But look at you now."

"I'm whipping up burgers now if you have time. This is how I plan to launch my chef career with a chain of Fatz Burgers."

"That's what I'm talking about. With this family there's always something new and positive happening. Destin, I need a new accountant. I believe this brother is cutting corners, or just can't handle this much cash flow because I think he has me paying too much in taxes."

"Do you have your paperwork with you?"

"Yes, let me grab the folder from the car. You need me to leave it for a few weeks?"

"I'm going to have someone look at it while you're eating your burger."

Booboo smiled, took the file from Destin, went to the office, grabbed a pillow, climbed up in the chair, and went to work. Forty-five minutes later, Booboo came out with the folder and handed it to Dream. He apologized for taking so long, then explained, "I had to look up some tax codes. For this quarter, your accountant was off by $160,000. I can go over it with your accountant if you like."

Dream looked surprised at Destin and then down at Booboo. He got his accountant on the phone and fired him. Dream said, "Whatever your next business venture may be, I want in. You guys know how to dream. By the way, I have a gift for DJ. It's a pure breed, male Giant Black Schnauzer from my dog's first litter. Since he is not here to receive this prestigious award, I will leave it in your hands, Mr. Booboo. I hope it's okay, Destin. I know I didn't ask you before I brought it over."

"No problem, we take all comers here, we turn down nothing but our collars."

CHAPTER 7

MO' MONEY

DJ signed a one-year, multimillion-dollar contract with Air Up Motor Cross Sports. He shot several music videos wearing their apparel that caused their brand and logo to sell out in stores. Air Up wanted to sign another deal with DJ for the same amount. Destin told them the offer must be at least $7 million or no deal. "We took a look at your numbers before you signed DJ, and after you signed DJ. You can afford it."

They declined, and DJ signed with Dirt First Motor Sports for two years and $10 million. The company put up billboards all across the United States and abroad. Dirt First made nearly a billion in sales of dirt bikes, helmets, gear, patches, and t-shirts. Anything that said "Dirt First" sold out in stores. Destin encouraged DJ, "If you can do that for them, you can do it for yourself."

Destin gathered his family, "Grace is coming home from rehab on Saturday. I would like for all of you to be here to support on her first day at home. It would mean a lot to me and Booboo. Also, on an official note, I will ask all of you who call Raphael Booboo to only use that name when we are home and not on the road. It opens the door for too many inquiries."

He called Faye to ask her and her new boyfriend to come by on Saturday for Grace's homecoming celebration. She agreed and thanked him for the invite.

Faye's new boyfriend, Morris, drove through Beverly Hills and couldn't get over the size of the homes. "Faye, I knew these houses up here were a nice size but this is ridiculous. Who are the people you know living up here, and what kind of work do they do? This is amazing. Thank you for inviting me."

"Turn right on this street and go through that gate," she directed Morris.

"That gate? We going to jail. Am I being punked?"

"No silly, park and get out of the car. You see all the cars here. I think we're late."

Morris got out, walked around to the passenger side, and opened the door for Faye. He headed for the front door when Faye pulled him around to the rear door. Morris said, "I should have known, we are the help. Is this your side job Faye? I don't like the feeling I'm getting."

Faye opened the door, waved at everybody, and introduced Morris to everyone. Fatz got up immediately and confronted his mother about bringing her side piece to his father's house. Morris recognized Fatz and was excited about meeting him, then extended his hand. Fatz slapped his hand down and asked him to leave. Destin got up and told him to stand down. He told Faye,

"Take Fatz outside and explain the situation to him."

"I thought you would have done that. Fatz, come with me. Let me talk with you."

"I thought you would have done that. Fatz, come with me. Let me talk with you."

Morris stood in the middle of the floor in shock, still holding his right hand from when Fatz slapped it down. Destin introduced himself and everyone in the house, including the camera crew. "Is this a reality TV show?" Morris asked with a puzzled look. "Something like that," Destin answered.

"Son, Destin and I are not together anymore. We split up while you were at USC. Please understand this. It's not Destin's fault."

"What did he do to you, mama? I know you loved him. You told me that."

"Listen to me, son. Destin asked me to marry him several times. The first time I told him I wasn't ready because of school and work. The second time, I told him I would think about it, but I never gave him an answer. The third time."

"Dang, mama! The third time?"

"Yes, the third time, I told him I couldn't handle life with cameras in my business morning, noon, and night. This is his dream come true, not mine. I didn't want to be on camera, always seen as the mad black woman and bringing down the show. Because of him, you have done so well for yourself, and I thank him for the man he raised you to be. I told him I trusted him with my prized possession, which is you. I could never compare another man to Destin. Because in my mind, there are no other men like him. I will always love him, as I told you before. I am a private woman, and Morris gives me that privacy. He lives a plain life. He is a college graduate with his own home and business. Destin asked me to bring him so all of you could meet him. So, please, son. Go in there and apologize to Morris and make him feel welcome.

Fatz signed the largest contract for a middle linebacker in NFL history - $120 million over four seasons, with $90 million guaranteed. He was offered $2 million an episode to do a spin-off show called Fatz Kitchen. Fatz already shot several episodes advertising his famous Fatz Burgers. Every player on the 49ers had been on the show and ate the Fatz Burger and Fatz Fries. They came in Hot, which he called Fire Fries, or the regular Fatz Fries. The Fire Fries were so hot that the container came with a disclaimer before eating. It created a worldwide challenge because so many of the guests on the show couldn't finish them.

Fatz purchased fifteen closed-down fast-food restaurants across the United States and converted them into Fatz Burgers. Every fast-food place that sold burgers within a mile of Fatz Burgers lost fifty percent of its business. Fatz offered a larger burger and more french fries than any other fast-food restaurant. Plus, he made special appearances allowing customers to take photos with him, tour the kitchen, and ask business questions. Initially, Fatz wanted to build brand-new buildings because he had the money.

Booboo showed him how much money he could save by renovating vacant restaurants instead. Fatz opened a bank account, depositing several millions, for Booboo to show his appreciation.

CHAPTER 8

MOVING ON UP

On the west side of Oakland, Fatz found a vacant strip mall for sale. He immediately asked Booboo to walk the property with him to make an offer. One of the buildings was an old hamburger stand called Kwik Way. Perfect! It allowed customers to drive up and park. Someone would come up to your car and take your order. Also on the lot was a vacant Mexican restaurant. Fatz thought this would be the perfect place to open his first Fatz Cuisine, an upscale restaurant that highlighted all of Fatz's cooking talent as he would do the cooking himself. He always thought ahead. The building next door to the Mexican restaurant was a carpet warehouse. It was not large but big enough to house what Fatz had in mind. He knew there would be long wait times to get into his restaurant. This area would be a waiting room filled with high-tech computers with mind-challenging trivia software. Worldwide art designs would highlight the finishing touches in the room. Raffles would be held every half hour, giving away gift baskets full of expensive wine, cologne, event tickets, and a complimentary meal to Fatz Burgers across the parking lot. The last building on the lot was huge. Fatz had thoughts of designing an inside golf course with long-putting greens and short chip shots, an area to work on one's drive off the tee against an automated screen.

Booboo loved the idea but couldn't understand why Fatz chose this area. He advised, "There is no big city for miles and slow growth in the demographic area. One corporation owns the whole strip. They're asking $18 million. Because of the things I just mentioned, let's offer $2 million and wait for a counteroffer. Fatz, you cannot use your name going into this deal. They will never come down on the price. Your name should never be mentioned. If they want a face-to-face, I will go and represent your company. I mean me and my mom." Booboo walked away with four buildings for $6 million.

DJ opened Cross'em Up Motorsports. He took his show on the road and would organize motor cross races from city to city. He teamed up with Fatz; he would be in charge of the vendors who were allowed on-site to sell food. Fatz food truck had the biggest stand at every show. Everyone wanted to try his food if they didn't have a Fatz burger in their town.

Cross'em Motor Sports became an enormous success because DJ offered categories for dirt bike racing. Different age groups. Female dirt bike and motorcross racing. Obstacle course challenges with great prizes. Sometimes, he gave away bikes along with cash and a trophy. Other times, he picked racing gear and a motorcycle. Contestants were signing up, years in advance, to compete in one of his races.

DJ still made music videos to accompany his rap songs, growing his brand into a billion-dollar business.

Destin sat down with Grace and Booboo to discuss him being a genius. "Raphael can calculate numbers in his head up into the millions. Did you know that?"

"No, but I'm not surprised. My father had the same gift. It skipped me and went to my son."

"You've never seen him calculate numbers? He's amazing and he loves doing it. I would like to put you and him on my payroll with your consent.

You two will be the company's accountants. You would have to be the face of the company because Raphael is a minor. By the way, Raphael has $15 million in his account. Courtesy of Fatz for saving him $30 million."

Grace agreed and took online accounting courses. She said it was as easy as taking a driving test.

Destin sent out a blast to people in the industry. He formed an accounting company for people like himself who were tired of being ripped off by the system because they didn't know the tax laws. The Dream was the first to respond. He sent a blast, confirming that he used Destin's company and that it was legit. The rap and sports world kept Raphael busy for the next two years. Grace set up the appointments, and he did the calculations. Raphael completed some of the most difficult, and complex taxes in an hour or less. The delay came when he had to attach the tax law chapter and verse to explain why they owed the money. So, in the future, they could do things differently. Raphael also gave recommendations on how to avoid these pitfalls at no extra cost. Grace was the contact person for the small company operating out of her home, six doors from Destin's home. No one knew Raphael, who was 11 years old at the time, was the mastermind saving people from tax fraud, tax invasion, and going to jail.

Athletes had the worst tax problems because of their bad money management. Destin didn't want Raphael to be exposed as the genius doing their taxes, but some needed private help. Hundreds of them were on their way to being broke if they didn't take control of their finances. Some local players came to the house and received hands-on financial training from Grace and Raphael. She would give the introductions and turn the class over to him. Grace was so beautiful that none of them cared about fixing their problems. They all made advances, offering to take her away from this life so she would never have to work again.

Grace quickly reminded them why they were there, and they could not give the world to anyone because they were only a few thousand dollars away from being flat-broke. The athletes quickly shut up and listened. Once Raphael began to speak, they didn't know if he was serious. How could this kid know all of this? Raphael kept their undivided attention when he pulled up their folders and displayed them on the screen. He broke down their wasteful spending and showed them a way to grow wealth through simple investing so they would never go broke.

The two of them became household names in the sports world. Daily, they received club and fifty-yard line tickets to football games and floor seats for basketball games, tennis matches, bowling, Olympics games, and track and field.

By the time Raphael was 15, he was a superstar. He always dressed nicely. Clients consistently sent him and Grace Rolex watches and other fine jewelry as a show of gratitude. Raphael was so busy that he never saw or spent time with DJ anymore. He kept the Schnauzer that Dream gave DJ because he was too busy to care for a dog. Whenever DJ sent for Raphael, he would always go because his work was remote and fast. DJ tried to make time for Raphael when he arrived, but it was not like the old days when they spent hours together. Raphael loved DJ.

Fatz would spend more time with Raphael because he needed business advice. Raphael loved Fatz, too, and managed his accounts and businesses. Fatz became his first client, besides sending all of the sports world his way. Raphael gained more and more exposure to the entertainment industry.

Once, Fatz and Raphael went unannounced to DJ's concert and sat on bar stools like the old days. Fatz had a bag with a Fatz Burger in it and began to eat just like he did when they were young. He and Raphael were shown on the big screen, and the crowd went crazy. The camera zoomed in on Raphael, and the women began bawling and yelling, "We love you." Raphael was rarely seen but often talked about.

CHAPTER 9

PEACE AND QUIET

While Raphael was gone with his brothers, the house quieted down. The reality show crew stayed busy filming in different locations. Now, Grace and Destin were finally home alone.

Grace always had tickets to sporting events, fine dining, spa treatments, gift cards, and Broadway shows. She took Destin on dates all the time. They enjoyed spending time together and never left each other. Destin thought, "This is what Faye was talking about; the private, quiet, quality of life. Too bad she didn't hang in here with me to enjoy these days." Destin and Grace became a couple. While Grace was in rehab, she asked Destin to contact a divorce lawyer, which he gladly did. Grace's husband did not contest anything; he gave her everything she asked for, and the divorce was finalized before Grace was released from rehabilitation. Destin wasted no time expressing his interest in Grace, and she confirmed the feelings were mutual. They were just another happy Hollywood couple.

Some time passed and Destin received a call from Faye asking if she could come up for a visit. He agreed and told Grace they would be having company soon. Destin suggested she put some clothes on because Faye would probably have Morris with her. Grace threw on a pair of Destin's sweats and a #24 Lakers Jersey. Faye came in through the kitchen like she always did, and to her surprise, no one was there except Destin and Grace. She asked, "Where are my boys at?" Chip, the dog, came out and rubbed his soft fur against her legs, and Faye squatted down and rubbed his furry face.

"I was expecting to see my family. Just you two are here? No camera crew, no filming, no one following you around from room to room? How long has this been going on?"

"We've been here alone off and on for about a year now. The house is quiet most of the time except for when Chip hears something and starts growling."

"I noticed you said, 'We've been here.' Meaning you two are a couple now? Oh! I see the matching sweatpants, one of you has on #24 and the other has on #8 jersey. I didn't notice that at first. Am I interrupting something?"

"Faye, you're always welcome in our home. Come sit down, and take your coat off. Why did you leave Morris outside? Invite him in. It's all love here."

"Morris and I are not together, Destin."

"Let me pour you some wine. Grace, would you like some wine?"

"I most certainly would. Do we get details, Faye? We're here for you."

"Faye sat down holding her glass of Chablis, right leg crossed over left, swinging her right leg just a little and staring hard at Destin.

Destin tried to lighten the atmosphere. "Whenever you're ready, let her rip tater chip." A stream of tears rolled down Faye's face. She stopped swinging her left leg and said, "How did I f*%^ this up?" Destin and Faye looked at each other with a tad bit of fear in their hearts because Faye reached into her bag when she spoke. She never took her eyes off Destin, slowly removed a folded-up piece of paper, and began reading it. It was from Morris.

> "Faye baby, I love you. I truly adore you. Your Jill Scott smile sends fire through my soul. I have never been as satisfied in a relationship as I am with you. I know you can't imagine where I am going with this letter. The trip we took up on the hill to meet your extended family opened my eyes to a world I never thought existed. They were living the lifestyle of the rich and famous. Everyone in that

house was rich and famous. I know better than to let what I see someone else has determine how I look at myself. I thought we could build our empire. I realize you went through a lot to get where you are today. One of the first things you shared with me was that you would never let a man take what you've worked so hard for from you. That phrase threw up a wall in my mind. I had a conversation with Destin while I was there. When he gave me a tour of the house, I was thinking you deserved to live here. She is that type of queen. I asked Destin how did he do this alone. He told me he dreamed it, and God made a way. He explained, 'My main goal was to move my son to a better neighborhood. I believe it would have been harder to get the okay to do certain things if I had a woman who was not on the same page. Faye is the perfect mate. If she trusts you, she will let you lead the way. Things fell into place when I decided to take care of these children who needed my love, support, and a fatherly figure. My dream was not about just me, but it included other people.

God opened doors, and I started stepping through them and never looked back.' Faye, I am moving out of your way to allow you to go and get the man that you love because I know it's not me.

Grace asked, "Can I get anyone some more wine?"

"Destin, what makes you think having to get the okay from a woman makes things harder to accomplish?" Faye questioned.

He fully answered her question. "For instance, DJ's mom, Nancy, believed in me when we first began dating. Whatever decisions I made, she supported them. When things didn't happen as I planned, she turned against me. There was a time when I was out of work. DJ was two. Every day, I got up and was on the hunt for a job. Nancy would say, 'When you gon spend time with your son?' I would line up interviews later in the day so I could spend time with DJ. If I came home tired and frustrated from being rejected and took a short nap, Nancy would see me lying on the couch and say, 'You lazy. I'm not going to be with no lazy man. Laying on the couch all day while I'm working.' I found a job, a respectable job. I was there for two weeks. Nancy called and asked me to take off early and pick DJ up from childcare because she has a hair appointment at 3:00 p.m. That's the only time Keisha could fit her in. My cousin was killed by the police, in an accidental shooting. The corner boys were having shootouts. I was having anxiety attacks, and my blood pressure was high. My mother called saying, 'Will you go find your father? He's out in the streets again.' I was sick for days. Nancy is on me, 'When are you going to move us out of the hood? If it ain't the police killing us. We killing each other. I can do bad by myself. I have dreams too.'"

"I tell you, when Nancy left us for the pursuit of happiness, it was the best thing that could have ever happened to me. My dreams became reality and so much more. I was shooting for a better neighborhood. God did it all."

Both Faye and Grace sat together, listening to every word Destin said. They were both thankful for him because of his contribution to their lives. They got up, sat on each side of him, and leaned their heads on each of his shoulders. Faye confessed, "I was going to accuse you of breaking up my relationship, but I know it's not your fault. I know the next time you invite me to bring a man over, I will come alone. Because I've spent so much time here in the past, it doesn't seem intimidating to me. But as I look around and see the space of a 9,000 square foot house, greeting a famous rapper, reality show star, professional football player, entrepreneur, and child genius, all under one roof will make you check yourself. And bring out the hate in a person. I love you guys, but I need to run. Thanks for listening and sharing."

Destin walked Faye out to the car; she wrapped her arms around his neck and hugged him tightly. She got into her 2023 Corvette Z06 and never looked back. Destin watched from the driveway until he couldn't see the car's tail lights anymore.

Grace pulled a blanket out of the closet, grabbed some cheese and crackers to go with the wine, and cuddled up to Destin to watch the Lakers game.

"Destin, did you think she was pulling out a gun when she reached in her purse for the letter?"

"Yes, I did!"

"I know, you almost broke my hand. You didn't ease up until you saw that white sheet of paper.

"I could see the pain in her eyes. She was hurting. Call and check on her. Please!"

CHAPTER 10

WHO KNEW?

Raphael was photographed with some of the most popular, beautiful models and women around the world. Most of his encounters were women pursuing him. Everyone wanted to know who was the young, handsome, mysterious man in the room. And how did he know all the wealthy people in the room or at the gathering? Raphael was flown all over the world, helping people with business offers, tax problems, and understanding tax loopholes. His accommodations were Presidential suites at many of the most luxurious hotels in every country. Time after time, he met with associates and left with a beautiful woman for the night.

He learned the game fast and never committed to the ones who came after him or offered sex like one would strike up a conversation. Raphael chose an Australian woman to be with him. She was the daughter of a wealthy Australian businessman he met months ago at a seminar in Paraguay. Samantha Golden was 19 years old, the same as Raphael, and they met on the elevator. When she found out he was in the suite across the hall from her father on the 45th floor, she invited him to eat dinner with them. When Horace, her father, saw the person she asked to dinner, he was pleased. Raphael was the keynote speaker at the seminar. Horace felt like his daughter was in good hands.

Samantha stood 5'8", with brown Australian sun-baked skin, brown eyes, and golden brown hair, half Aborigine and half white. Raphael was falling in love for the first time. As a supermodel, her photos covered all the major magazines for women's health, beauty, and fitness. She became a runway model at 13 years old. Now a young adult, Samantha goes and does whatever she wants, and she wants to be with Raphael.

DJ had a hard time on the road traveling with the Rap Legends Tour. Security was lazy and allowed the crowd to jump up on stage. Mostly women, but their job was crowd control. DJ was twenty minutes into his show when a girl climbed onto the stage and tackled him from behind. In a matter of seconds, security grabbed the lady off of him and removed her from the concert. But not before she cut off one of DJ's braids. He didn't notice and finished his show. DJ walked backstage and received high-fives and fist bumps from the other artists when one of them noticed a braid missing.

He was tired of the whole rap game after four Rap friends were shot in their city. They posted their location online and were met with gunfire.

As DJ sat in the barbershop waiting for his haircut, he decided to go with the nappy look. There was nothing wrong with an image change.

He also put in a call to Fatz to travel with him as a private bodyguard for his last four shows.

After thinking hard about ending his Rap career, DJ called his father and expressed his desire to get out of the Rap game. He knew his father would have words of wisdom because he retired several years prior. Destin shared, "Son, if the thought of retiring is in your head, it's time to stop." DJ thought he would hear a long speech about giving up your dreams. Why quit now in your prime? You will regret it later. But no, instead, he heard go with your heart.

Fatz was having the newly purchased buildings renovated in Oakland when he received a call from DJ. "Hey Fatz, I need you."

"Where are you?"

"Denver, Colorado"

Fatz hung up the phone and headed to Denver. It was rare that DJ called him for anything besides Fatz didn't like the sound of his voice on the phone. The renovations were going well on his buildings, and he wouldn't be needed for some time.

"My brother, it's good to see you," said Fatz.

"Thank you for coming."

"You decided to turn the braids loose, I see."

"No, someone decided that for me. That's why I called you here. Security at the rap shows can't contain the crowd and a woman jumped on the stage, attacked me, and cut one of my braids off. I only had six. I need you to watch my back while I'm on stage."

"Take the barstool."

"Exactly, but not for long. I have four more shows and I am done with Rap. I told Pop's and he agreed. It doesn't have to be a life-long gig."

"What are your plans for the future?"

"I will continue growing my brand with Cross'em Up Sports. I still love racing and that to me is a better high than rapping."

DJ's last concert ended, and as far as he was concerned, so was his Rap career. Fatz returned to Oakland to check on his new project. DJ started shooting a big video for Cross'em Up Sports and brought in one thousand extras to be in the stands for the commercial. It was an all-day shoot. Afterward, everyone ate food provided by DJ and was paid $20 for their participation. DJ was having a "Meet and Greet" with everyone when a group of local boys began shouting and yelling at him, "You ain't shit." He yelled a few words back and ran up to them. Security stepped in and stopped the action before the crowd got wind of it. They ran the group of locals off, but DJ was pissed. He looked around for his crew; they were in the faces of some women, so DJ took off on his motorbike.

By the time his crew noticed, fifteen minutes had passed. They heard about the incident with the local boys and took off on their bikes to find him. The video shoot was up in the hills, where the races were held, away from the residential areas. A series of winding roads led up to the location. His crew hoped the reality show crew was following him and recording his footage.

Everything DJ did and wherever he went was recorded; this was part of his personal crew's job. They all rode with cameras on their helmets because DJ always seemed to do something spectacular.

DJ came out of a winding road to see all six local boys sitting on their bikes and talking. From his rearview mirror, he saw the reality show film crew coming but still a way back, coming around the winding road. DJ flew by the local boys, and they immediately followed after him. He wanted to fight them but did not know if they had guns. He pulled over into a dirt field because they couldn't keep up with him. DJ got off his bike with an extendable Billy Club in his hand. They surrounded him and started talking trash. DJ wasted no time and began swinging his club, knocking them off their bikes. It turned into a wrestling match, and they got DJ to the ground. The show crew decided to film the footage rather than break up the fight. DJ's motocross crew showed up, and joined the fight, punching and pulling the guys off him, and beating the local boys down. They grabbed their bikes and took off. DJ remained on the ground, lying on his back, laughing just a little because it hurt after being punched and kicked.

DJ, the motocross crew, and the Reality show crew all stand around talking and looking at the footage of the fight when DJ says, "Let's ride." They still had a mile and a half of winding road before they reached the main highway. They loved leaning into the curves until their knee would touch the ground. That was the rush that DJ lived for every day.

DJ, the motocross crew, and the reality show crew stood around talking and looking at the footage of the fight when DJ said, "Let's ride." They still had a mile and a half of winding road before they reached the main highway. The crew loved leaning into the curves until their knees touched the ground. That was the rush that DJ lived for every day.

Darkness fell, and the winding road was poorly lit. DJ always had on his helmet, gloves, padded jacket, and pants. He took off like a rocket, with his crew trying to keep up. DJ overtook a couple of cars by crossing into oncoming traffic. Each time he did this, it extended the distance between him and the crew. DJ felt the pain from being kicked and punched in the ribs, back, legs, and head. He slowed up because he was feeling dizzy, and it was dark. His crew was three cars behind on their bikes when DJ took off again, passing two more cars on the opposite side of the road and slowed down behind a cube truck. DJ swung out and punched it to get past the truck because the oncoming Jaguar was approaching fast. He could slide through as he had so many times before, but it would be close.

Melvin, the driver of the Jaguar, was a middle-aged white man, a college graduate, hard-working, and vice president at the bank he worked for in Colorado. He was 6'2" with a slim build and balding down the middle of his head. Arrogance prevented him from being popular with the ladies, but the Jaguar filled in where he was lacking. Melvin dated women who liked his car and not him. Today, he dined with Emily to celebrate her 21st birthday, spending $150 on dinner and drinks. He planned to take her to his place, get in a session, and take her home with a win. But Emily wanted to see what his Jaguar could do around those curves. No problem for Melvin, that's why he bought the car, to help him get the woman. Melvin had a few drinks earlier but was not drunk by his standards. He took on the curves like a champ, and Emily asked to drive while sliding her hand between Melvin's legs. He grinned the Joker's smile and looked over at her. Emily screamed, and her eyes increased to the size of ping-pong balls. She pointed, "Motorbike!" Melvin had crossed into oncoming traffic.

DJ would have easily split the Jaguar and cube truck if Melvin hadn't crossed the line. He tried to jump the bike into the air to soften the blow, but Melvin was coming too fast. DJ flipped up and into the truck, smashing the front windshield. The truck driver slammed on the brakes, causing DJ and the bike to slide across its roof, and land on the ground behind it. The bike landed on DJ while his head bounced several times on the pavement. The truck smacked Melvin's Jaguar and crumbled his front end. Immediately, the airbags deployed, saving the lives of Melvin and Emily. Someone from the show crew called 911.

"This is 911. What is your emergency?"

"Multiple vehicle accident. One motorcycle down. Multiple injuries on Winding Turn Lane."

Within minutes, the winding road was blocked off and looked like a crime scene. DJ lay motionless and was the first transported to Aspen General Hospital. Melvin and Emily were taken to the hospital together with minor cuts and scrapes. Most of their injuries were from the airbag deploying. The cube truck driver was questioned and allowed to leave. He suffered no injuries, but his truck had a smashed windshield. DJ's motocross crew stood on the side of the road, arguing about who should call Destin. None of them could break the news to him. Two of the show's cameramen went with DJ to the hospital on the orders given by Arnez Harris, the show's producer. He gave them direct orders not to let DJ out of their site and keep the cameras rolling.

Destin received a call from one of the cameramen riding in the ambulance with DJ. He told Destin that his son had been in a motorcycle accident and was being transported to Aspen General Hospital. He made some calls and arranged for a helicopter to take him and Grace to

Aspen General from Los Angeles. On the way, he reached out to Fatz in Ohio. Fatz scheduled for a helicopter to take him to the hospital. Grace called Raphael but had trouble reaching him. DJ was in the emergency room for forty-five minutes by the time Destin and Grace arrived. They were delayed by another helicopter landing on the hospital's helipad.

The passenger of the other helicopter was none other than the famous reality show producer Arnez Harris of the nominated reality show *Pastor Swap*. Mr. Harris caused a contestant to be slapped by her husband for allegedly cheating. This incident caused hot grits to be poured down the back and head of the pastor, resulting in him being hospitalized, having a heart attack, and dying. The same Arnez Harris hired people to create havoc on the set and almost caused one of the contestants to be arrested and almost shot by the police. Arnez will stop at nothing to keep the title "Reality Show King."

When Destin and Grace entered the hospital, Arnez was barking orders to everyone, including the hospital staff. He insisted that his cameras be allowed in the emergency room when Destin asked, "What are you doing? There will be no more cameras taping this show until we find out my son's condition. Get your men and your cameras out of here." Destin and Arnez stood face to face, arguing, until they heard screaming. Fatz walked in and said, "Sounds like there is a problem here."

Arnez quickly turned to Fatz, "Help your father understand how important it is for us to have this footage for the show."

"There is no more show until we find out if DJ is ok."

"Son, we're keeping this quiet," Destin looked at Fatz.

"Yes sir."

Arnez took out his phone, walked out of the area, and sent a text detailing the accident and the health of DJ. Within an hour, chaos had erupted at Aspen General Hospital. A post of DJ, lying in all his gear, was viewed on TikTok more than 1 million times. People all over the world reposted, asking, "Is it true that DJ is dead?" News trucks and teams began to arrive. Extra security was posted on the emergency room floor to keep the media out.

As the family paced in the waiting area, Fatz grabbed one of the camera crew who rode with DJ to the hospital. He showed Fatz the footage he had of the accident. He told Destin to contact DJ's motocross crew, who wore the headcams, to show him the whole footage because they were right behind him when it happened.

Destin's cell phone began to ping non-stop. Then Fatz and Grace's phone began to ping. The Rap world sent messages saying, "We mourn with you."

"We lost another good one."

"Ride or die."

"Was he killed?"

"Not little DJ."

The Dream sent a text, "I'm on my way. I'm there for you. Whatever you need my brother."

Fatz received messages from football players, "We grieve with you. We love your little brother."

"Sorry for your loss."

"Praying for your family brother."

"May he rest in peace." Over and over, these messages never stopped.

When Grace's phone pinged, she thought Raphael was finally returning her call. But no, it was every entertainer in show business who knew DJ from Raphael and Grace. She received the photo from Raphael that everyone was referencing and showed Destin. "The photo is not true. Come to Aspen General Hospital in Colorado. Take a helicopter and land on the roof."

Destin turned his phone off. He saw Arnez Harris on his phone, talking and texting. "Did you do this?"

"Not me, I'm praying that he's ok." The doctor came out to speak to Destin, and Arnez ran up to him, asking to see DJ.

"Are you the parent?"

"I'm the parent, doctor. I'm Destin Balin."

Arnez told his crew to get ready. They were about to roll DJ out of emergency.

"DJ had a bad accident. From what I was told a car crossed into his lane from the opposite direction, knocking him up against a cube truck that was behind him. He and the bike slid across the roof of the truck and landed on the ground. The bike landed on DJ but he remarkably suffered no broken bones. DJ is unconscious, he was knocked out when he came in and has not come out of the coma. We are preparing to transport him to ICU."

The lower floors of the hospital are filled with fans from all walks of life. Motor cross world, sports world, and entertainment. A candlelight visual has begun outside of the hospital. The street is blocked off. Nothing moving in or out of Aspen General.

Security asked Destin if he had a guest list because over 300 people were claiming to be family trying to come up. He gave the security guard the names.

"Destin Balin, father."

"Grace and Raphael Santiago, mother and brother."

"Fitzgerald and Faye Cummings, brother and mother."

"The Dream, Carl Lane, uncle."

"Robby Rock, uncle."

"Nancy Clark, mother."

The security guard paused, "Mr. Destin, you have three mothers listed."

"It's complicated."

"Reality show life?"

"Exactly!"

"Can you have security remove this film crew?"

"We thought they were with you."

"Their names are not on the list."

"Understood."

With only the family in ICU, the room became quiet. Almost scary. Grace began to cry and turned her face into Destin's chest. Fatz sat quietly, talking to himself. Destin said, "It's a waiting game from here. Let's get comfortable. We don't know how long this may take. Some staff brought more chairs into the room, and Grace requested another bed.

The Dream walked into the room two hours later and woke everyone up with boxes of chicken, barbecue, and Chinese food. "Is anybody hungry?" Tired, sad, and irritated, they all joined hands and prayed along with The Dream as he prayed aloud for DJ. Fatz made the funniest comment, announcing that he could not eat his competitor's food. Everyone smiled and lightly chuckled, then devoured the food.

He told them it was like arriving at the airport with the number of helicopters landing and taking off from the helipad. "My chopper waited in line for forty-five minutes before being signaled to land. And, thanks for having my name on the guest list. I didn't know how many people I had to pay off to get in here. Did you know about 3,000 people are outside this hospital blocking roads in every direction because DJ is here?"

Destin said, "Some fool posted a photo of him laid out that set off a firestorm. We think we know who did it, but we will deal with him later."

Security had no choice but to close the hospital until they could clear the street. Only emergency victims and guests on Destin's list were allowed to arrive by helicopter. All others were turned away. By 2 a.m., the streets were cleared, with a couple of hundred fans still waiting for DJ to wake from his coma.

Faye arrived at 7 a.m. the next morning; security alerted Destin that his son's mother had arrived. Fatz said, "It's Faye." She walked in with two big bags and a suitcase. "Fatz asked me to stop by the house and pick up a change of clothes for everyone. I also picked up toothbrushes, shaving razors, deodorant, socks, and extra sweatshirts and pants. Also, Grace, I got you, girl. Here is your bag."

Fatz groaned, "Mama, no food?"

She slowly walked over to DJ's bedside and pulled back the curtain. Faye stared at him, grabbed his hand, and looked at all of the monitors, numbers, his heartbeat, and IV drip. She turned to look at Destin, then kissed DJ on his forehead and collapsed on the floor. Fatz ran over, picked up Faye, and carried her to the empty bed. Grace called for a nurse, who was already en route because she watched the whole thing through the window.

Raphael was discovering love in the Australian Outback. Samantha had taken him on a six-day luxury learning trip through the Outback. She wanted Raphael to learn about her people and where she came from. He was sheltered from a hard life, and backpacking through the desert heat in 100-degree temperatures was taking its toll on Raphael. Because of the location, there was no cell service, and Grace was unable to notify Raphael that DJ was in an accident.

Six days later, Raphael and Samantha reached Sydney, Australia. Raphael's cell phone was blowing up in his hand. Samantha looked at him and asked, "Did someone die? Whose blowing up your phone?" Raphael had 190 messages. The first photo he saw was of DJ lying on the ground with his bike on top of him. Raphael cried uncontrollably as he read several condolence messages before reading the one from Grace. She told him to come to Aspen General Hospital in Colorado quickly. He went online to book a flight and found nothing available for two days. With tears still rolling down his face, he asked Samantha's father for help.

Horace Golden asked, "What's the problem, Raphael?"

"My brother has been involved in a motorcycle accident, and I need to get to Aspen, Colorado."

"Aspen! That's where they took DJ from Cross'em Up Sports?"

"Yes, he's my brother."

"OMG! I love him. I watch his races all the time. Let me call my pilot; he will gas up the plane and get you there in about sixteen hours.

Raphael called Grace, told her he was on the way, and asked how DJ was doing.

"He's in a coma, son."

"He's not moving at all?"

"He hasn't moved in the last seven days, baby."

Raphael started crying again, his eyes now red and swollen. Samantha threw a blanket over him, and he slept the rest of the way to Colorado.

Arnez Harris pleaded with Destin to let him stick a camera in DJ's room. When Destin denied it, Arnez reminded him that he was still under contract with the reality show and had not shot anything in days. Destin replied, "How about a one-on-one interview with each of us? I cannot guarantee you it will go well, but I will ask them to do it."

He went into a room set up with cameras and lighting. He sat on a bar stool, and the make-up person dabbed at his face to remove some of the shine.

"How are you feeling?"

"Tired, scared, and angry."

"Do you think DJ will come out of the coma?"

"You're about to get slapped."

"Let me rephrase. Did the doctor say when DJ may wake from the coma?"

"No."

"What are your plans going forward?"

"I don't know."

"Thank you, Destin, I know that this is a very difficult time for your family. Please send The Dream in. Dream, you've been involved in DJ's life for some time now. What inspires you about this family?"

"If you notice, there is always a positive vibe in the atmosphere when I'm around them. There is no jealousy or fighting. One alpha male is leading his family. Everyone is playing their part. You see, Destin has two women here with no drama and one on the way. The man has been blessed by God, and he's living a dream."

Security notified Destin that Raphael, one of the people on his list, had arrived. Grace ran to the ICU doors to meet him. They embraced, and she rubbed his face and looked him in the eyes. "I need you to hold it together in there, son. You've never seen DJ like this before. He has tubes hooked up to him to monitor his heartbeat and blood pressure. They're feeding him through a tube, so prepare yourself. Who's your friend?"

Raphael walked into the room, spoke, and hugged everybody. He pulled back the curtain and looked at DJ's thin, frail body lying in the bed. Raphael pulled off his shoes and climbed into the bed with DJ. "I told you he was going to do that," said Fatz.

Once again, Arnez Harris begged Destin to let him get this footage. Destin conceded, "The best I can do is sit a camera in there. Not a cameraman, but a camera."

Raphael was five when he met DJ. He stood four feet tall compared to DJ at six feet. He began to talk to DJ, "Remember when you used to ride me on your back? And the time you had to pick me up because I was afraid of the big dog? How about when you would pick me up so I could swing on the monkey bars?" They lay in bed side by side when Samantha, left in the hallway, entered the room. She spoke to everyone and stood right in front of the camera, blocking the live feed. Raphael continued to talk to DJ; he had never seen him like this. He reminded him of how he would hide in the house, receive a call from some girl, and stop looking for him. Raphael talked for over an hour and finally grabbed his hand. "Why won't you wake up and talk to me? Please don't leave me. I will die."

Samantha broke down in tears, hearing Raphael express his feelings to DJ with everyone else in the room. Fatz walked over, hugged Raphael, and helped him out of bed. He was having trouble breathing, and Fatz didn't want to see him pass out as Faye did. Samantha moved from in front of the camera and sat beside Raphael on the bed. Neither one of them said a word.

Arnez was in the interview room and had no idea that Samantha was blocking the camera placed in the room by Destin. The scene with DJ and Raphael was heard but not seen. The visual would have been monumental. That was valuable footage that he could never recreate.

CHAPTER 11

NANCY'S RETURN

Sheila sat in the cubicle across from Nancy at work. Sheila was Nancy's best friend in high school and the reason she landed the internship at the hotel in Vegas. Unlike Nancy, Sheila attended college out of high school and earned her degree.

When Nancy went off to college, she pursued a Master's degree in Management. In every textbook, Nancy placed a photo of DJ to make her smile. Nancy interned at a hotel chain headquarters in Los Vegas. She was bright, well-liked, and sexy as hell. Her long, thin frame with bowed legs caused problems when she walked around the college campus. Her smile was inviting and made you feel like you had a connection with her. So many men made the mistake of thinking they could offer money and gifts just to take the prize to bed. Nancy took pride in herself. Always smelled nice, dressed sexy, and sometimes too sexy for the office environment.

Relax Suites, the hotel chain, had a partnership with some of the colleges. Thousands of interns came through their program to learn the industry business. Other businesses offered the same, but Nancy loved Vegas. She was the only intern that made $200,000 a year. Her job was to work half the day as a receptionist because this position prepared her to multitask and keep the office running. The other half of the day, she did the job. Nancy demanded such a large salary when the company's CEO noticed her and decided he could persuade her to be with him. She was thirty-nine years old. Mr. Marks was a seventy-two-year-old, balding white male, tall, arrogant, healthy, and strong for his age. Nancy never met him before and had no idea who he was.

The Christmas party given every year, was held at the MGM Grand Ballroom. All of the employees came because the gifts were incredible. Bonus checks were distributed, and prizes like luxury trips, cars, and house appliances were given away at the party.

Mr. Marks saw Nancy talking and laughing with co-workers and joined in on the conversation. His photo was in the foyer on every floor, but not everyone paid attention to things like that. Nancy greeted him and shook his hand. Her smile along with her firm handshake, excited Mr. Marks. Nancy wore a Black silk dress with most of the left thigh and back exposed down to her butt. He lustfully looked at Nancy's back, saw the curve and the size of her backside, and couldn't help himself. Mr. Marks cuffed the bottom of Nancy's butt in his hand and held it there until she jumped. Nancy drew back her arm and got ready to knock his teeth out until Sheila whispered in her ear.

On January 3, Nancy sat in the HR office with Sheila viewing a video of Mr. Marks cuffing her butt at the Christmas party. He requested a sit-down meeting with Nancy and Sheila.

"Have you shown this video to anyone else?"

"No."

"Good, I would like for it to stay that way. If you agree to the amount, you can both be on your way."

Sheila was already a full-time employee training Nancy. Both of their salaries increased to $200,000 a year as long as that video never surfaced.

Sheila was sitting in the cubicle across from Nancy and said, "I think this is so sad, what happened to this young man? He was doing so well."

"Who are you talking about?"

"Don't you watch the news? This young man has been in a coma for over a week after a motorcycle accident."

"Oooh, girl. A coma. For over a week?"

"He's a handsome young man. His name is DJ."

"What? What did you say his name is?"

"DJ, here look at my phone. You know him?"

Nancy grabbed the phone and looked at the photo, and it fumbled in her hands.

"Nancy, you, ok? What's wrong?"

"I think that's my son."

"Girl, I didn't know you had a child."

"Is that article from Oakland?"

"Says here, he's in Aspen, Colorado. General Hospital ICU."

"Aspen, Colorado. I have to leave."

Security stopped Nancy, "Good afternoon, may I help you?"

"Since when does security question someone walking into a hospital," she asked with a puzzled look.

"Ma'am, we have a celebrity here who was injured in a motorcycle accident two weeks ago. We have a guest list for the people allowed to see him. If your name is on the list, we have a special elevator to take you up to his floor."

"Nancy Hussle. I'm his mother."

"Are you mother 1, 2, or 3?"

"I am his god-damn mother! Am I on the list or not?"

"Take this elevator right here to the left, young lady. Press button 11."

"Which mother am I? These fools gon' make me lose my mind up in here. Destin has all his hoes listed as the mother. What kind of mess is he trying to pull? I wish one of these hoes would try to claim my son."

"Hello, Mr. Destin, Nancy Hussle is on her way up."

Destin said, "I need everyone to move to the next room. Now! Nancy is on her way up and I want her to have some privacy with her son."

Nancy stopped at the nurse's station and spoke with the charge nurse on the floor.

"You have my son DJ on this floor?"

"My name is Nurse Martha, and yes, we do. DJ is in this room right in front of you, just pull back the curtain. Please allow me to give you his status. DJ is in a comatose state. His blood pressure is normal; his heart rate is a little slow but stable. He has lost a lot of weight because he is not eating solid food. He is hooked up to a lot of monitors and an IV drip. He's doing ok, we just need him to come out of the coma."

Destin appeared in the doorway of DJ's room while Nurse Martha was still speaking. Nancy caught his movement and pointed her finger at him while listening to the nurse. Destin stood with his arms crossed, swallowed hard, and prepared himself for this typhoon headed his way.

Nancy walked into the room with her finger still pointed at Destin. She pulled back the curtain and saw DJ lying in the bed, hooked up to several monitors. She covered her mouth, then accused Destin, "I asked you to do one thing, and that was to take care of my son." He walked out of the room, closed the door behind him, and watched through the window.

"DJ, it's mommy. You know my voice, don't you?" Nancy grabbed his hand, staring down at her only child, she began to weep.

"Lord Jesus, forgive me for all of my sins so I may boldly come before your throne of Grace. If there is anyone I have a fault with, please forgive me and forgive them." Nancy then saw Destin through the window.

"Now Lord?" Nancy signaled for Destin to come into the room.

"I apologize for what I said to you earlier. I don't believe that this is your fault. I see he is grown and you raised him without me to this point. I am sorry for leaving you and DJ. May God continue to bless you and your other women. Please leave the room." Destin never said a word. He stepped out of the room and continued watching through the window with his arms crossed.

Arnez Harris was excited to have this footage. He wanted more interviews while he had the rest of the family together.

"Robby Rock, how are you doing through all of this? Can you tell us what's going to happen with DJ if he comes out of the coma?" Everyone in the room looked at Arnez and blurted, "If!"

"Let me rephrase that. When he comes out of the coma."

"My spirits are low. I want to see DJ up and dancing, laughing, and entertaining. That's what I would like to see going forward. DJ is my nephew. I saw him two days after he was born. I can't say anymore." Robby got emotional and walked out because he couldn't stop crying.

Fatz sat on the stool and warned, "If you ask me anything crazy, I'm going to beat you with this stool."

"Please, speak freely Fatz. No questions."

"DJ is my younger brother. I love him as much as I love my mother. When his father took me in, I was accepted as a son and there was no jealousy in the house. When I went to college, DJ was happy for me, but cried when I left because we had not been separated since we met."

"One question, Mr. Fatz. What happens if he doesn't come out of the coma?"

He got off the stool, "Didn't I tell you don't ask me no stupid questions." Fatz hurled the stool at Arnez and then chased him out of the room.

There was a lot of talk coming out of DJ's room. If anyone looked through the window, no one was there but Nancy. Her voice could be heard down the hall. She had fallen on her knees praying. She took off her jacket and stretched out underneath DJ's bed, navy blue pantsuit and all, face down, praying for her son to come out of his coma. The three nurses assigned to this area had never heard a prayer like this and joined hands. Everyone in the adjoining room came out to hear what Nancy was saying. By this point, Nancy had broken out into unknown tongues. No one knew what she said, but Faye understood; she prayed in this manner most of her life. Faye took Grace by the hand, and they agreed with whatever Nancy was saying because they knew she was talking to God the Father.

The room became quiet for a minute. Nancy had been praying for a half hour. DJ opened his eyes for the first time and looked around the room but saw no one. Nancy was still down on her knees, and the curtain was closed. DJ closed his eyes. Nancy stood up, wiped the dust off her clothes, put on her blazer, and pulled the curtain back. Everyone dispersed; no one could look Nancy in the face. She asked for some water and went into the bathroom. When she came out, Raphael was at his bedside, holding DJ's hand and crying. Nancy wondered who this handsome young man was holding her son's hand, crying this hard. She pondered, "Oh no! Who are you, young man?"

"I am Raphael Santiago."

"I know you. I know your name. What is DJ to you?" She thought, "Please don't say lover. Please don't say lover."

"He is my big brother."

"Wow, ok. Destin has lots of kids, I see."

"Just me, Fatz, and DJ. Who are you?"

"I am DJ's mother, Nancy. And did you say Fatz? Like in Fatz Burgers?"

"Yes, that's him standing next to Dad. DJ is squeezing my hand. Here, feel."

"I knew you could hear your mother's voice." Nancy waited for the head nurse to come in.

Nancy had so much to learn about this family. So many questions she wanted to ask. Arnez Harris approached her and asked if he could interview her live for the show. Nancy looked at Destin, "What is this? Who is this man? And is he serious right now?"

"Nancy, we have had a reality show for years. The only reason they are here is because we are under contract. If you don't want to be interviewed, it's ok."

"What is he going to ask me?"

"I don't know."

"You know I still have that ESO (East Side Oakland) in me. If he gets out of line, I'm going to bring it."

"I would expect nothing less."

She sat down in a chair because Fatz busted the stool when he threw it at Arnez. Nancy put on her charming smile. This was her first time on television, but she was ready.

"Nancy, the mother of DJ. Where have you been?" Arnez started the interview. Her smile went from an elegant smile to a frown that caught Destin's eye. He yelled out, "No!" But it was too late. Nancy jumped out of the chair and slapped the fake grin off Arnez Harris' face. In shock, he fell backward in the chair, trying to get away from Nancy. "You want an interview? Bring your ass back in here. I have a hundred more answers just like that one. How he gon ask me, where I've been?"

Destin told the family the doctors would be running tests on DJ for the rest of the evening now that he was awake. "One of us can stay for support and the rest should take this time to get some rest. We will start shifts, and anyone who wants to come can. But I want someone here at all times." Raphael quickly said, "I will stay."

"What about Samantha?"

"Please take her home with you. She needs to meet all of you anyway. She can sleep in my room."

"Samantha, it's up to you."

Destin made arrangements for two helicopters to pick up everyone and transport them to Los Angeles, except for Fatz, who was going to Oakland.

Nancy wrapped her arm around Robby's arm and began chatting while waiting for the helicopter. Robby knew her from junior high and high school. For a short period, they lived on the same block in elementary.

"Robby, who are all these people?"

"Ok, let me break it down for you. Faye is Fatz's mother."

"Fatz is the Fatz Burger man?"

"Yes, and Grace is the girlfriend and Raphael's mom."

"Raphael, I know him or I should say, I heard of him. Robby, who is he?"

"Raphael happens to be a child genius. Grace was in a bad situation and Destin kept him while she was working through her issues. I should say

DJ took care of him. It seems like DJ needed a little brother because he took Raphael everywhere. Spent time with him like he was his very own child. Taught him how to ride a bike, swing a bat, and taught him all about motorcycles. It's funny, but Fatz and DJ came together similarly."

Robby continued. "Let me break this down for you. When you left, Destin's life changed immediately. He made a Rap record that became number one on the charts for a month. This led to a record deal. Destin rented a home for him and DJ in the Oakland Hills. This is where DJ met Fatz. Faye also wanted to move her child to a better neighborhood. Fatz and DJ became best friends. He was over every day because Faye was going to school at night and Fatz was always home by himself. Destin took him in and co-raised him. A reality show got hold of Destin's story and loved it because he was different from most rappers. Arnez Harris, one of the biggest and most well-known reality show producers, offered Destin a multimillion-dollar contract. Faye allowed Fatz to move with them to Los Angeles. The *Destin Family* reality show is the most watched television show, other than *The Kardashians* in the last nine years."

"Are you kidding me? This is a dream."

"There's more. Fatz became a fan favorite on the show because he would eat hamburgers at Destin's rap concerts, and DJ would get up and dance. This led to him creating most of the dances you see today. DJ began making money, got involved with motocross sports, and became the champion in his age group. This led to endorsements and DJs making millions of dollars. DJ decided he wanted to be a rapper like his father and began traveling with The Dream. DJ started his own motocross company selling apparel and bike accessories. This made DJ a billionaire before he was 20 years old."

"Fatz had become a college football star, then a pro football star. Then he was crowned fast food king. Now, he's a restaurant owner.

"Where did Raphael come into the picture?"

"Raphael was home with Destin when he discovered the child could calculate numbers up to the millions in his head. He became a tax consultant, with the help of Grace, to most entertainers, sports athletes, and businessmen, worldwide."

Nancy remembered, "That's where I know him from. We had to attend a conference where he was the keynote speaker. The women were asking him to sign their clothes, purses, and table napkins. The boy was amazing."

"He has lived with Destin since he was five. He calls Destin 'Daddy', and me, 'Uncle Rob'. DJ means the world to him, if DJ was to not make it, neither would Raphael."

"Everyone is welcome to stay here. We have plenty of room. Faye, please stay for dinner before you leave. I know you have to work in the morning. Nancy, you can sleep in DJ's room. It's down the hall, turn left, and go through the double glass doors. Passed the theater room and across the patio."

"Are you kidding me? This house is that big."

"Come on girl, I will show you. Grab your bags," said Faye.

"Faye, you were dating Destin?"

"Yes, for a minute."

"What happened?"

"It was me. I didn't like the cameras being on us all day every day. I like my privacy."

"All those hips and boobs you have, I thought he would have kept you."

"I kept him coming back. I had him sore and tired. I put it on him several times a day while I was here. I had to give him enough to hold him over because I was living in Oakland, and working in San Francisco. He would walk with a limp for several days after I left. Ask Robby, he'll tell you. Destin saved me. I know I would have fulfilled my dreams, but he made my journey so much easier. He was God's gift to me. I'm rushing home from work, cooking Fatz something to eat, and rushing back out the door to get to class. Four nights a week. One day, Destin walked into my life, and a weight lifted off of me. I trusted him with my son, just like you did. I love that man, and nothing, and nobody will ever change my mind."

Nancy was listening to Faye as she unpacked her clothes, and tears began to swell up in her eyes.

"What about Grace, what's her story?" she asked.

"Grace was his neighbor. She was living on this street before Destin moved here. I will not speak for Grace, only she can tell her story."

"Wow, that smells good. Who's in the kitchen cooking? Where is the kitchen? Which way do I go?"

"Chef Royal," replied Destin.

"Chef! You have a chef? What else do you have Destin?"

"That's it. He came with the house. The show paid for him. When he formed a spinoff reality show with Fatz, his popularity increased and he was on every show in America and abroad. He's like family now. When Chef Royal is in town, he stays at Fatz's house in the valley. Fatz and DJ bought me this house as a surprise birthday present several years ago."

"Destin, I need to be here for DJ's recovery. I have a job in Las Vegas and a condo there, but I need to be close to my son. Will you help me?

On the advice of Raphael, Fatz decided to open the drive-up burger stand in a West Oakland strip mall before the other businesses remodeled. "Fatz Burgers in a community like this will outperform all of these other businesses put together. We have a grand opening and ribbon-cutting ceremony and drop the prices for the first month. After that. raise the prices slightly, but keep them much lower than your competitors and give away discount coupons."

Fatz Burgers had a line of cars wrapped around the corner on the grand opening day. There was nowhere to park in the lot or on the street. The west side of Oakland had shown up in support of Fatz Burgers. Destin, Faye, Grace, The Dream, Raphael, and Samantha had flown in to support him too. Raphael advised, "Fatz, get a few of the employees to take orders from some of the people lined up on the street to try and clear the main highway."

"We don't have any available people."

"Come on Samantha, we're going to work."

Raphael grabbed Samantha by the hand, wrapped a Fatz Burger apron around her waist, placed a Fatz Burger hat on her head, and gave her an order pad and pencil. They both went out to the street and began to write orders. Fatz noticed that traffic was not moving as fast as they thought, so he brought out the big grill and started making his famous burgers right there in the parking lot. Destin put up a roadblock so no more cars could enter. Fatz had Faye start the oil in the deep frier, and the rest of the team bagged burgers and fries and gave them away at no charge. The ribbon-cutting ceremony was at 10 a.m.; the last burger was given away at 9 p.m. Fatz did not make a dime, but he won the people of the west side of Oakland.

News trucks were onsite interviewing the staff at Fatz Burgers and some of the patrons.

"How did you enjoy the food at Fatz Burgers?"

"I have never eaten a Fatz Burger, it was big and juicy. The fries were hot and greasy, just like I like them."

"How did you enjoy your dining experience today?"

"We didn't have to pay. We walked up and received a bag. We took a picture with Fatz while he was cooking."

"How was your experience here at Fatz Burgers?"

"I'm glad they decided to do the giveaway because the line was an hour long. I had the munchies and ran out of the house without any money. Thank you, Fatz!"

"Sir, how was your experience here?"

"I wanted to try the Fire Fries. I like hot and spicy food, but they gave me regular fries and no drink. How am I supposed to eat a burger and fries with no drink? I don't think they thought this plan out. They were not prepared.

"You heard it here first. Cherita Jenkins, WKXT News, West Oakland, signing off."

Nancy moved her life to Los Angeles. She gave her two-week resignation letter to Mr. Marks personally, which he gladly accepted. He apologized again to Nancy for his behavior and ensured she understood a job position was always open, but it would be at the regular pay rate. Nancy signed a document agreeing to his terms if she decided to return. Sheila helped Nancy clean out her cubicle and took the rest of the day off to spend with her friend. She had so many questions for Nancy.

"How's your son?"

"Not good, in and out of the coma."

"Where will you live? Are you getting back with his father?"

"No, I will be living in the Valley at his stepson's house."

"In the Valley! At his stepson's house? Is he married? How does he have a stepson with a house in the Valley? It's expensive in the Valley."

"Girl, you're not going to believe this."

"Believe what?"

"Let me talk. Girl, everyone in his house is a millionaire. DJ, my son is a billionaire. Sheila! Sheila, are you ok?"

"I'm trippin. I thought you said your son is a billionaire."

"Yes, girl, he is."

"That answer's my next question. I was concerned about how you were going to give up the $200,000 a year. But billions trump everything. So, is the house in the Valley nice? It's a five-bedroom, 4,500 square foot house with a three-car garage. I have to share it with their chef. But he's never there."

"What? Do they have a chef? What else do they have?"

"That's the same thing I asked Destin."

"If you live in the Valley, where do they live? Meaning everybody else. Since you said everyone in the house is rich."

"The main house is at the top of Beverly Hills."

"Nancy, you may step down. I have no other questions. I ought to punch you in the mouth. You didn't know all of this was going on?"

Grace called Destin from DJ's bedside. "Destin, DJ is talking in his sleep."

"What's he saying?"

"It's in another language. I don't know what language it is. One of the nurses here speaks several different languages. She's been called to come up to his room."

"I don't believe this is happening. You're witnessing a miracle."

"I know, but why."

"Is the camera still on in the room?"

"Yes, I think so. I see the red light on. That means it's recording."

"Thank you, baby, I am on my way."

Raphael was in Australia with Samantha. Sam could tell he was not the same person she met nearly six months ago. He was often in deep thought and shed tears at a moment's notice. She tried to comfort him by singing; Raphael loved to hear Samantha sing and loved it more when she tried to dance. He curled up in a ball, laughing at her dance moves. Raphael would turn on a video of DJ to show her how it's done. Samantha thought his demeanor was depressing and that he might be suicidal. In an attempt to brighten his spirit, she played a video of him as a small boy, and DJ was practicing a TikTok dance routine with him. He started to smile, looked at Samantha, and grabbed her by the hand, and they danced to the video. Raphael never had rhythm, and neither did Samantha. So, they bumped into and fell over each other until they were tired.

"Nancy, are you in LA?" asked Destin.

"Yes, I arrived yesterday with the rest of my things."

"Come to the hospital as soon as possible."

"Is he awake?"

"Nope, he's doing strange things. I don't know how long he will be doing this but we are recording him. A helicopter will be waiting for you."

"A helicopter? Ok, bye! I have to get used to this life. I don't know about getting in a helicopter."

Grace greeted her first at the hospital. "Hey, Nancy!"

"Hey Grace, Destin."

"Nancy, he's been talking in his sleep."

"Ok, what's so special about that?"

"Shhh, not so loud! Listen to him. It's in another language. This is the third language he's been speaking in."

"In school, I learned to speak three languages fluently. I would teach DJ new words every morning on our prayer call. Maybe this is a download of the things we discussed because he misses his mommy. Oh my God, this is a miracle. What do we do?"

"Wait it out."

Destin received a call and left the room so he would not disturb DJ. A troubled look overcame him as he listened and ran his hand across his head. He looked at DJ through the window, walked over to a chair in the hallway, and sat down. Destin hung up the phone and put his face in his hands. His loud, deep cry caught the attention of Grace and Nancy, and they both headed to the door. Grace looked back at Nancy, "I got him." Nancy gave a fake smile and went back to DJ's bed. She understood but kept watch through the room window.

"Destin, baby. What's wrong?" Grace stood in front of him, pulled him into her stomach, and cradled his head.

"They killed him." Grace cried, too, because it had to be someone close. She was afraid to ask whom he was referring to.

"Dream, he was shot and killed in his hometown of Gary, Indiana." Grace exhaled and continued to cradle Destin's head against her stomach.

CHAPTER 12

WHAT A TRAGEDY

"Pop, pop, pop" was the sound heard coming from the mother's house of the rapper called The Dream. His real name is Carl Lane. It's been reported that Carl, The Dream, was at the top of the Rap game. He was the richest and most successful. With several movies under his belt, Carl had just signed another multimillion-dollar deal to star in his very own reality show beginning this fall on TV ME."

"Witnesses say Carl was here visiting his mother before he began shooting his reality show in Los Angeles. Witnesses also say people are always watching his mother's house because she didn't want to leave the hood. It looks like Carl drove his Phantom home, easily recognized by its color, and caught the attention of some of the thugs in the neighborhood. Carl was leaving his mother's house, at approximately 2 a.m., when he was shot three times in the chest. His body dropped right here next to where I was standing. You can still see the blood stain on the sidewalk. The sad note to this is that there were no witnesses. Carl leaves behind nine children. This is Cherita Jenkins, signing off from KPOK, your local news channel."

"We just spent the whole day together at Fatz's grand opening. We talked for hours about his reality show contract. He made a deal with all six of his babies' mothers to allow him to keep the kids so they could be on the show. We celebrated all day, and now he's gone. Ain't no coming back from three to the chest," sighed Destin.

"When we did his taxes, he mentioned having a will written up. I hope he took care of that. I told him I would help him write it," Grace said.

"I hate to say this, but I'm glad DJ doesn't know what's happening. It would send him into a coma."

"Come on Destin, let's go and sit with DJ."

Fatz was in a Los Angeles gym working out hard. He didn't work out as much as he would like to; so he was going hard at it. Breaking news interrupted the current TV program and reported that the rapper, The Dream, had been shot to death. One of the jail-house-looking guys in the gym commented, "That's what he gets. All of them damn rappers are gay."

"I know that brother, he isn't gay," replied Fatz.

"Maybe you're gay."

"You got the right one brother."

"You're not my brother, your brother is gay."

Fatz hit the guy in the face and with one punch, knocked out his teeth, busted his nose, and blackened both eyes. Fatz looked around, and no one said anything. No one came over to see what happened. It happened so fast. Fatz thought it was best to leave the gym while the getting was good.

Grace was sitting on Destin's lap with both arms around his neck, loving on him, when TMZ showed a video of Fatz arguing with a man in the gym and then knocking him out. Destin jumped up with Grace still wrapped around him and said, "Turn up the volume. I want to hear what was said."

"Oh my God! That's the worst thing this fool could have said. Talking about Dream and DJ. Why did Fatz hit him? This guy doesn't know either one of them. Shit, Faye will be calling any minute," added Grace.

"I don't know what's going on. Seems like our family is under attack. Call and check on Raphael. No need to tell him what happened if he doesn't already know."

Nancy let out a small scream. DJ sat up straight right in front of her. Destin and Grace rushed to his bedside and saw him sitting up. Destin asked, "Son, do you know who we are? DJ wiped his eyes and nodded his head. He turned to his right and saw Nancy. He blinked his eyes several times, then slowly wrapped his arms around her neck. DJ spoke out loud for the first time since being hospitalized, "My mama." The family lost it. They hadn't heard his voice in almost a month. Nancy hadn't heard it in years. She hugged him too tightly, and the nurses had to come in and separate them. Destin smiled, "It's about time we've gotten some good news. Hell yeah! I'm happy now! Look at God. Won't he, do it?"

Grace called Raphael to tell him the good news but got his voicemail and hung up. She didn't want to leave a message; she needed to talk to her son, hear his voice, and know he was okay.

Raphael was doing fine. He and Samantha were working on their rhythm, not dance steps. She cradled his head with her legs wrapped around his waist. Raphael came up with a beat that both of them could move to. Their bodies were in sync, and the rhythm was easy.

"Raphael, are you going to answer your phone?"

"Nope, it's my mother. Probably checking on me."

"What if it's about DJ?"

"Fatz or my father will call. Now you're messing up the rhythm. Let's start over."

Fatz's lawyers informed him that the guy he hit was willing to settle out of court. They shared, "Looks like he has an extensive arrest record and several open cases that could put him back in the penitentiary for a while. We came up with an offer of $50,000 with paid medical bills also. If you agree Fatz, sign here, and this mishap will be behind us."

The headline read, "The Dream Owed Several Gangsters Money." He was involved in an underground drug smuggling organization and on the run from child support. The Internal Revenue Service was hunting him down, and he was under investigation for several shootings.

"Still no leads or witnesses on who killed Dream?" asked Grace.

"There's not one word in the article about how he stopped the dispute between Thirsty Ma and Cum Get It. Or how he stopped the crowd from rioting after the police shot G-LO-B. He saved a lot of lives that day. Dream brought the South and Canadian Rappers together. He sold out Coachella. This was the first concert held after Covid-19 restrictions were lifted. Remember when he donated a couple of million dollars towards after-school programs for inner-city youths? How could someone who has done so much be talked about so horribly in the media?"

Faye remembered, "He did several advertisements for Fatz Burgers. He was wearing a Fatz Burgers T-shirt when he was shot.

"I hate reading the paper. They paint a picture for the world to read that isn't true. You read what they said about DJ. He was fleeing the scene of a crime. They will do whatever it takes to make the story sound juicy and sell papers," Destin rightfully criticized.

"The Dream hasn't been dead a week and they have begun to slander his name. Do you think we can do something to help change that?" asked Grace.

"Hmmm, not without getting ourselves investigated. We don't know everything about his dealings. Let's see how things play out. If there is an opportunity for us to speak on his behalf, we will."

"Are we attending his funeral?"

"Oh no, that is going to be a circus. And there is a shooter on the loose. I'm glad DJ is not able to go. He would be sitting in the front row as part of his family. I'm not mentioning this to him until after it's over.

"DJ is sitting up, and he is alert. His eyes are wide open, and he has begun to smile. Those are all good signs of recovery," reported Head Nurse Martha.

DJ asked Nancy, "Were you coming back if this didn't happen to me?" She paused for a long time before she spoke. DJ looked her in the eyes with the most innocent look on his face. Nancy could see the little boy in him even though he was in his twenties. "DJ, I know you think I left you. You were my reason for leaving." He frowned and crossed his arms.

"That's exactly what your father would do. But let me finish. We were struggling with income and I was immature. I used you as an excuse to leave your father. He was doing his best. I know this. But I wanted more and he couldn't give it to me."

"But why no contact with me? No Aretha Franklin?"

"DJ, I'm still your mother. Don't interrupt me. Let me finish. I messed up so badly that I couldn't live with myself. I met a man that could fulfill my dreams and followed him. He led me down a dark path that was hard to return from. I couldn't reach out to my parents because they would have told me what a fool I was for leaving you. I was too embarrassed to ask your father to take me back. I thought he was still struggling to make ends meet. I took for granted the family time we spent teaching you how to ride your bike, the picnics at Alameda Beach, feeding the pigeons at Lake Merritt, and trips to Know Land Park Zoo. I didn't know I was living a dream back then. Life was easy."

"Again, why no phone calls, no more early morning prayers? No *I Say A Little Prayer For You*? Do you remember the words?"

Nancy started singing….

"The moment I wake up before I put on my makeup,

I say a little prayer for you.

And while combing my hair now

And wondering what dress to wear now

I say a little prayer for you."

"DJ, I went to jail for a couple of years. My life turned upside down as soon as I left our family. Your uncle Robby told me how God opened up a window and poured blessings all over you and your father. And it seems like the same for everyone your father came in contact with."

"You seem to be doing fine now, mama. You dress nice, smell good, and you sound educated. I still don't understand."

She sung another verse…

"Forever and ever, you stay in my heart, we will never part.

Oh, how I love you.

Together, together,

That's how it must be to live without you.

Would only mean heartbreak for me.

I say a little prayer for you."

"DJ! I, like so many other people, decided to take God seriously in prison. Life was hard for me in jail. When I gave my life to Christ, my belief had to be tested. But I kept the faith and other women saw me going through my tests and followed Christ. DJ, I had to fight in jail. Women tried me because I was pretty and had never been to jail before. I gained a reputation fast for beating women down until I came across this lady called, "Pretty Red." I never met a woman that pretty who could throw hands as she did. That got me sent to the hole for 30 days. I sat, talked, and listened to my Lord. Each time I came out of the hole, I was wiser, stronger, and sharing the Gospel of Jesus Christ with the same women I had fought. My life began to change and I was released on a technicality. I enrolled in school. I graduated with a four-year degree in three years. I received an internship at a major company last year. Everything was going well, DJ, until my boss thought it was okay to touch me."

"Did you hit him?"

Nancy started another verse….

"I run for the bus, dear

But while riding I think of us, dear.

I say a little prayer for you.

At work I just take time

And all through my coffee break time,

I say a little prayer for you."

"DJ, I was cocked, locked, and loaded. I had my finger on the trigger and I was going to pull it. But no, I did not hit him. My best friend, Sheila, whispered in my ear that she captured the whole thing on video. We could sue the company. God had a ram in the bush. You probably don't understand."

"Yes, I do mama. Genesis 22:13, he made a way because you were headed back to the joint."

She continued the song…

"My darling, believe me, for me

There is no one but you, please love me too.

I'm in love with you.

Answer my prayer,

Answer my prayer baby."

"Wow! DJ, this happened four months ago. I'm just now getting back on my feet. I quit my job and humbly asked your father for help.

"He answered your prayer. Didn't he? That's what happens when you say a little prayer for me. I love you, mama."

Nancy finished…

"My darling, believe me.

For me, there is no one but you.

Please love me too.

This is my prayer.

Answer my prayer now baby."

Five rough-rider-looking young men showed up in DJ's room. Nancy jumped up immediately. Destin calmed her, "It's ok. Down girl. These young men are from DJ's crew. This is Rod, Kevin, Larry, Victor, and Daryl. They were with him the night of the accident. They have never seen before footage of the accident."

"How did they do that?" asked Nancy.

"We have cameras on our helmets. We video all of our adventures. Here look at this. The reality show crew doesn't have this footage," Daryl shared.

"DJ, I didn't know you fought that day," his dad commented.

"Looks more like an ass-kicking," Nancy chimed in.

"They jumped me."

"Ok, I see you went around the truck. The Jag crossed over into oncoming traffic. They said you caused the accident."

"What are you talking about?"

"You're being sued, son. Once they found out who you were, their testimony changed. They said you swung out into the oncoming traffic when you were overtaking the truck. They were countering to keep from hitting you. But this video clearly shows something different. DJ, were you trying to jump the bike over the Jaguar?"

"That was the plan. Because they were coming in at an angle and I was coming out of my bend, and couldn't snatch the bike up high enough to clear their car. Plus, the speed they were going didn't give me enough time."

"Wow, they knocked you into the windshield of the truck!"

"Because I was in the air already when they made contact."

"I see your back tire is what shattered his windshield. He locks up his brakes causing you to slide over the roof of the truck and hit the ground. Don't look at that, Nancy."

"I just heard your blow-by-blow description of what happened. I'm ok. Oh, DJ, baby! Oh no! Oh, DJ, baby. Never mind, I don't want to watch it."

"DJ has two singles left on his last album with no video. Take this to Robby and have him work his magic. This is going to change the game. Come with me, Nancy. Let DJ and his crew talk."

"Hey, Booboo!"

"Hey, Fatz!"

"Our brother is awake, talking, laughing, and asking a lot of questions. One of his first words was where are Fatz and Booboo. So, we need to get there as soon as possible. I have two meetings I cannot miss this week. The walkthrough for the remaining buildings is on Thursday, and I want to cut the ribbon on Saturday. I don't want everyone to rush out here again since we cut the ribbon on the Fatz Burger restaurant together."

"My mom had been texting and calling me but I assumed she was checking on me. Now I feel stupid. That's great news. I will see you soon brother." Raphael hung up the phone and had that look in his eyes.

Samantha said, "Oh no. Not again."

"No, I'm fine. I'm going back to the hospital. DJ has come out of the coma and he's asking for me."

"Ok, I have a list of things that I need to do that I haven't done. So, if it's ok with you, I'm going to stay here."

Destin, Nancy, Grace, and DJ sat in the hospital room. Nancy flipped through a women's health magazine and shared a few interesting articles with Grace. Destin and DJ were discussing Fatz and Booboo when his phone began to ping nonstop.

Grace asked, "What's going on? They're blowing me up too."

"I got nothing," Nancy said.

"Oh God, look at the photo posted of DJ," Grace fumed.

"Oh shit! It says 'He's alive. But may never walk again.' This is posted all over social media."

"Destin, who's posting this about my son?"

"I think it's Arnez Harris."

"What are you going to do about it? I know you're not going to let this ride. If you're scared, say so. I will handle it."

"Nancy, shut your mouth. You're not gon' do a damn thing. I got this!"

"I'm sorry, I forgot, you're the man. I will stay in my place. That's my bad. My mouth gets me in trouble."

Grace motioned to Nancy, "Come with me. Let's sit in this other room and get an understanding."

"What's that?"

"This is Fireball Whiskey, mixed with lemon juice over ice. Takes the edge off. Go ask the head nurse for a cup."

"I know Destin used to be your man, and you had your way of handling him. But he is no longer your man. And you will not raise your voice to him. He deserves respect. We all respect him in this house. Faye treats him the same way. If she doesn't agree with him, she will check herself before stepping out of line. Destin is a loving and caring man. His gift in life has been to help others, and we respect him as the alpha male. He looks out for all of us and will address any issue that arises up."

"I understand, forgive me. I am learning to keep my cool. I had a man named James who schooled me on the game of life and talked me into fulfilling his dreams. He was different from Destin. Gave me things I dreamed of, but it came with a price. I began selling myself for him. I let him get in my head. When I came to myself, I told him no. I wasn't going to do this anymore. Before I knew it, I was on the floor looking up at the ceiling. One day, He left me in one of his lavished apartments, and I began straightening up because I'm a neat freak. I found four of his guns stashed throughout the apartment. He came in the door with this good-looking brother named Maurice. He looked at me and handed James a wad of money. I said, 'I'm not doing it.' He raised his arm, and I reached into my waistband. He paused and began yelling at me. I pulled the gun's hammer back. He raised his hand, stepped towards me, and I wrapped both hands around the pistol grip and said, 'Act like you're going to say something.' He acted, and I reacted. I put a bullet hole in the middle of his forehead. I looked at his fine-ass friend and asked, 'Do you still want some ass?' I served three years for killing him."

"Wow, girl, I had no idea! I understand, my husband spoiled me rotten until Raphael was born. He had me partying with these friends of his that did cocaine all the time. I got hooked and was left to care for Raphael alone. He left plenty of money in our account, and I continued to get high. Until, one day, I passed out, woke up and Raphael was gone. That was the first time DJ and Destin brought him to me. The second time I passed out, I hit the floor face first and knocked out my tooth. I broke a bone in my nose which blackened my eyes. I was on medication and still doing cocaine. Raphael left the house and I had no idea he was gone for six hours. Destin brought him home again and encouraged me to get some help. I had no choice but to accept. When I say he deserves respect, I mean it. I cannot stand by and listen to you raise your voice at him. He is respected and loved in this house."

Nancy apologized to everyone and sat by DJ's bed. A wild-looking young man came to the door, and Nancy stood up and put her hand in her purse. Destin asked, "What are you doing? Relax, he's Cloud 5. He was on tour with DJ."

"Didn't they just shoot a rapper to death? And why do you call yourself Cloud 5? Was 9 too high?"

"Yes, you get it. Mr. Destin, there is a gang of people forming outside of the hospital now that it's been posted that DJ is awake. I just happened to make it in before the police blocked the doors, and I saw a helicopter landing on the roof."

DJ got excited because he knew it was either Fatz or Booboo. In they walked. Tears from all three men caused Destin to break down and cry. He shared, "Grace, you and Nancy come with me. Grace, go buy some guest books, so people can sign them and leave words of encouragement. I think the crowd will settle down if we do that. The hospital has been patient with us. Let's do some crowd control. Fatz, you and Booboo come down and help as soon as you can. There's a lot of people down there, and a lot of them are your fans too."

Robby shared details of The Dream's Funeral service. "Flowers, limousines, police, friends, and family were all around the Gain Bridge Fieldhouse Arena in Indianapolis, Indiana, the birthplace of The Dream. The small parade held for him was interrupted by rain and cold weather. There were still people lined up to see him as the funeral car rolled by. No one this great had ever come out of Indiana since the Jackson Five. The Dream had become a hero to state's inner-city youth. He was proof that the system couldn't hold you back if you tried. Long and short speeches were given in memory of him. A small statue of The Dream was unveiled at the Boys and Girls Club where he used to play basketball every day. Approximately 1,000 rappers were in attendance. Four rappers came together and did a Cypher on behalf of The Dream. At the end of the ceremony, he was laid to rest in an undisclosed location. The funeral was beautiful."

"As you can see, we have our hands full here. I think it was no coincidence that it leaked that DJ was awake the same day as the funeral. I don't think it was Arnez this time. I believe they wanted as few celebrity rappers at his funeral to give the impression he was not loved by his people.

"This is going to get worse Destin. Everyone I ran into at the funeral was surprised to see me, thinking I would be here at the hospital. Hundreds, if not thousands more, are coming to show their support by the end of the week."

"That's why we're down here now having fans and friends sign a guest book letting DJ know they were here. Plus, his fans get to meet other celebrities up close and in person."

A television report redirected Destin's attention. "Hey look, on the TV." Breaking news. "The shooter of The Dream has turned herself in to authorities. Her name is Sandra Jackson. Sandra admitted to shooting and killing The Dream after hearing all the false accusations against him. She was one of his many children's mothers. Sandra said she was mad at him for coming to town and visiting one of his other babies' mothers and not her. She gave herself up because she didn't want her 'baby's daddy's name drug through the mud. After all, he was a good man.' Her words, not mine. This is Cherita Jenkins, signing off from KXTV-12 in Indiana."

"Wow, that's good and sad news! She did the right thing by coming forward and turning herself in," commented Robby.

CHAPTER 13

MY III SONS

The next voices DJ heard were of his two brothers, Fatz and Raphael. He saw them walk by the window and began to wiggle his feet like a newborn. "Come here, little fella."

"My name is not little fella, it's Booboo."

"I was talking to Fatz."

All of them fell out with laughter and embraced in a group hug. Nancy had never seen all three of them together and wanted to know how three strangers bonded into brothers. The laughter and stories they told never seemed to stop. DJ asked

Raphael, "How did you two end up on the same helicopter together?

"Fatz had another ribbon-cutting ceremony and I didn't want him to do it without a family member being there. I'm glad I saw it firsthand. Fatz went way over the budget I set for him."

Nancy wondered, "DJ, something is going on with Booboo because he used to answer my emails within one minute of me sending them. I sent him all the estimates and receipts, but he never responded.

"Booboo, it's obvious you're having sex. I noticed it in the way you walk. You stick your chest out, and now your voice is deeper and you look buffed. All signs of having sex. Booboo, do I know her?" she probed.

"She was here when you were sleeping. She stayed at the house hoping that you would wake up. I flew back to Australia with her two weeks ago."

Nancy slid her chair over to the bed. She wanted to know her son's brothers and bond with them as a stepmother, to be someone they could trust and confide in. "How are you three so close?"

"I will go first," Booboo said. "When I met DJ, he started taking care of me from the time he climbed off his bike. He took me to his house, cleaned me up, and fixed me a sandwich. He said, 'I don't have a little brother, but I have a big brother.' I agreed to be his little brother, and he never let me down. He picked me up from school, made sure I looked clean, and had on nice clothes. You know kids can be brutal. Because DJ was well known, that made me the most popular kid in school.

Fatz was already in college but came to pick me up when DJ couldn't make it. After a few pickups and drop-offs from Fatz, my teachers and principal loved me. He asked me on the first time, 'Do I need to beat up anybody?' I was allowed to be on the sidelines with the team during the home games at USC as long as DJ was with me. I had the best childhood that a child could have because of these two and Dad."

"My story is different. DJ and I both moved to a neighborhood with no friends. We met after school. We were the only two guys waiting on the bus going to the Oakland Hills. The bus would drop us off halfway, and we had to walk the rest of the way. I was heavy then and would wait for my mother to pick me up from school. That's how I got on the football team. DJ had a moped and asked his father if he could ride to and from school. Dad drove us at first and then decided to let DJ take the moped. Here's what bonded me and DJ together. I was so much bigger than him that it was hard for him to handle the moped. DJ climbed on the back, and I drove him to and from school, and everywhere else we went. Dad was so kind-hearted, he bought me a moped for my birthday. I knew a good thing when I saw one. I became a part of a family you saw on television and YouTube."

Fatz continued talking. "Here's a story that we never told. Booboo doesn't know this story either. We were living in the Valley house and wanted to see LA from the streets. We had the camera crew take us because we were always riding in limousines and being chauffeured. The dropped us off in Watts. We walked and they followed close behind but out of sight and kept the cameras rolling. We walked through Crypt neighborhoods and were noticed immediately. A gang of Crypts came up to us asking us questions and wanted to take pictures with us. An OG came up and ran the small guys away. Asked us if we were being recorded. We told him yes, and he said, 'Get the hell out of here little niggas. We can't have our operation on primetime TV.' We autographed some stuff for his kids and kept it moving. Now Ms. Nancy, you know something Dad doesn't know."

They all laughed. Nancy thanked them for opening up to her, expressed how she valued their stories, and promised never to tell. They all came in for a group hug and a selfie. Everyone was smiling in the photo except for DJ. Nancy asked, "DJ, baby, what's wrong?" He didn't respond or move, and his eyes were closed tight. Fatz shook him gently. Raphael ran and got the head nurse. "Everybody, clear out of the room. Let us do our job," the nurse ordered. They rolled in the heart monitor and an AED.

Nancy headed down to the lobby with Grace and saw thousands of people walking around outside. Lots of celebrities, sports figures, and fans. "Destin, can you quiet everyone down, and get their attention? I need to make an announcement." He saw the seriousness on her face and felt Grace sliding her hand inside of his, gripping it tightly. "Grace, what's going on?" She whispered in his ear. Destin took off running toward the elevator. Nancy waited for him to quiet the crowd and turned around but saw no one but Grace.

The elevator was taking too long, so Destin headed for the stairs. Fatz and Raphael came down in the elevator while Destin ran up to the eleventh floor. Destin had no type of athletic activity in the last nine years. He could not breathe by the time he reached the fifth floor. Gasping for breath, Destin hung on to the stair railing and continued his journey to the eleventh floor. Fatz and Raphael were looking for him in the lobby when Grace told them he went up on the elevator. Fatz yelled, "Everybody quiet!"

"Thank you, Fatz," Nancy said quietly.

"Everybody, my brother is back in a coma and my father is missing. If you see him, he's needed on the eleventh floor."

Fatz and Raphael entered the elevator for the eleventh floor. When they exited, they saw Destin on the floor holding his chess and gasping for air. One of the boys turned to the doctor, "Doc, what happened to my father?"

"Raphael, he has suffered a slight heart attack."

In the room, Raphael sat in a chair between the two beds, turning his head from left to right. "I pray that both of them recover."

Nancy began praying right outside of the lobby, and Grace asked everyone to join hands. The prayers were so loud that many of the patients in the hospital went to their room window to look down. A news helicopter received notice that something was happening at Aspen General and was circling the building.

Fatz whispered in Grace's ear, and she immediately screamed. Nancy felt Grace's hand pull away and saw her running back into the hospital. She looked at Fatz, deep into his eyes, as if to search his soul. She thought DJ passed away. Nancy started to stumble and fell over. Fatz swooped her up and carried her inside. While she was tended to, Fatz announced that Destin had suffered a slight heart attack. "Please continue to pray. We are in a family crisis right now, and your prayers are keeping my family alive."

Arnez Harris was jumping up and down with much pride. He poured a Scotch and saluted himself, then looked at the number of viewers watching live. Arnez shut down all other programs. *The Destin Family Reality Show* was the most-watched show in television history. The new addition of Nancy, the drama queen, had been a blessing. "And I don't have to pay her. I am the G.O.A.T!"

Nancy sat quietly in the wheelchair, being rolled into the elevator and back upstairs. She looked through the window and wondered why Destin was lying down in bed. He's still a lazy nigga she thought. Grace was on one side holding his hand, and Raphael on the other. "Is he looking for sympathy while our son is laid up about to die? I'll be damn!" Nancy slowly walked over to the other side of DJ's bed, with her eyes on Destin, and a scowl on her face.

She whispered to Raphael, "What is your daddy doing?" He looked deep into his mamma's eyes. "He suffered a heart attack." Nancy's scowl left immediately, and her face began to crack. Stress lines overtook her face, and forehead veins protruded to her nose. She never felt so foolish. Destin was the first love of her life.

"Stressed out, confused, hurting, and has suffered a heart attack. I'm judging him as if I have no faults." Nancy leaned her head back in the chair and bawled uncontrollably. No one in the room paid her any attention.

Security hit Destin on the radio to tell him that a helicopter landed on the roof and he had a visitor. Fatz jumped up, "I forgot my mama was coming." They heard the elevator ring, and Faye stepped off with a huge bouquet. He met her, and they embraced. She handed Fatz the flowers, asking him what was wrong with his face. As he began to answer, Faye was already walking by the room window. She saw Nancy sitting in a chair sobbing, DJ hooked up to monitors, Raphael holding his hand with his head down, and Destin in another bed holding Raphael's other hand. Grace held Destin's other hand, rubbed her hand across his head, and massaged it gently.

"Let's see if I can figure out what has happened here. Nancy has done or said something stupid. That is a pity cry. I can tell by the vein running down the middle of her forehead. Poor DJ looks like he slipped back into a coma." Faye walked to his side, grabbed his hand, and kissed his forehead. She walked around the bed, bent down, lifted Booboo's head, and whispered gently, "Take care of your brother. He's going to need you when he comes out of the coma."

"Yes, Ms. Faye. I will."

"Oh my! Did Destin have a heart attack?"

"Yes, mama," answered Fatz.

Faye stretched across Destin's still body to hug Grace, who was stretching across the bed to meet her. She motioned across the room. "I'm glad you were here Grace to take care of our man because that one over there is a hot mess, and needs to pull herself together."

"Mama!"

"Fatz, let's go to the next room to chat. I want to know what's going on with you."

"How are you feeling? A lot is happening here today."

"I know, it was supposed to be a celebration with DJ coming out of his coma. We were talking and laughing and he went dark. Lights out. Dad was in the lobby doing crowd control. He found out and tried to run up eleven flights of stairs. His mind was telling him yes, but his body was telling him no. He suffered a slight heart attack. The doctor said along with having the stress of DJ on his mind, his blood pressure was high, and lack of exercise took him out of the race."

"Shoot, I was gon offer him some."

"Mama!"

"When Nancy found out that DJ slipped into a coma, she fainted. I caught her and brought her inside the hospital."

"What's she in there bawling about?"

"You don't want to know."

"What's going on with the project in West Oakland?"

"I did the ribbon cutting yesterday and flew here today with Booboo. He surprised me and showed up to give support. I love that little man. Mama, I discovered a vacant lot behind my lot. Thirteen acres for sale for a reasonable price. While Booboo was there, we looked up comparables in the area and made an offer. I think that area is going to be Fatz Headquarters. I want to build a hotel that's equipped with all the luxury of the big city. I can get a contract with some of the sports teams to stay here when they're in town. Who knows Mama!"

"I like the idea, son. Create your little city within a city. And, stop fighting son. You know I don't like that. Makes my nerves bad when I see you on all the news channels and sports channels, and you don't play anymore."

"It wasn't a fight. I knocked his ass out. No one will speak badly about DJ or anyone else in this family while I'm around."

"Son, can we go somewhere and have a drink? I wasn't expecting all of this madness."

Fatz and Faye found a small bar within walking distance of the hospital. Most of the patrons were there for the same reasons they were. In need of an outlet to get away from the drama. They decided to sit at the bar. One other gentleman sat alone drinking a beer and following it up with a shot. He commented on everything that came across the TV screen. Faye drank a glass of red wine, and Fatz had water with lemon. The smooth sound of Jazz was playing in the background. The bartender recognized him and asked, "Are you Fatz?"

"Yes, I am."

"I attended USC while you were there." The guy at the bar immediately tuned in to their conversation. "You left USC early and I was just entering. I attended all the home games. You still look like you can play."

"Once you enter the pros, the game becomes a lot faster, and with that comes the injuries."

"Can I ask you what are you doing now?"

"It's been a rocky road. I graduated last year, but I need to do another two classes. My stepfather owns this bar, so I am helping out until the fall semester begins."

Someone at one of the tables asked, "Can you turn up the TV? That's the Cross'em Up Sports kid. The one that was in the accident.

Fatz turned back to see who was speaking when Faye began to pat his hand. He slowly turned back around. "I love that kid. My son and I watch his show every week. He's wild on that bike." The gentleman at the bar added, "His wild ass is fighting for his life. Look at his little dumb ass flying around those cars. And for what? He made a rap video off of it. What an ass hole!"

The bartender cut his eyes over to Fatz and saw him about to make a move on the man. He advised, "Sir, can you keep your opinions to yourself? Please!"

"Isn't this a bar? Where else am I supposed to voice my opinion? The barber shop is not open this late."

"Sir, it sounds like you're letting the alcohol speak for you."

"Come on Fatz! Let's go," said Faye. The bartender told them no charge for their drinks. Fatz left a $100 tip in the jar anyway. As they left their seats, the gentlemen made one other statement. "The news said he slipped back into a coma. His ass is as good as dead."

"Fatz, hold my purse."

"Mama, are you going to the bathroom?"

"I'm about to slap this fool."

Faye took two steps toward the man. He saw the blow coming before it hit. She caught his left jaw with four diamond rings on her right hand and knocked him off the bar stool. Faye had his flesh embedded in her rings. The man jumped up to see 6'4", 275-pound Fatz holding a purse and said, "Oh, shit! Hey, man, I don't want any trouble with the LGBTQ community. I'm sorry."

"Fatz, I feel like dancing," Faye smiled.

"Inside Club Hammer, Faye and Fatz hit the dance floor. She was smiling and having a good time. He was happy to be with his mother. It's been a long time since they've been anywhere together. Right there on the floor, Fatz and Faye made up their dance steps. He watched DJ do it several times at home, so he took Faye by the hand, and she followed his steps. A crowd started to watch because Fatz was well-known everywhere. Before long, the crowd picked up on the steps, and now it was a party. Fatz bought the club a round and headed out the door. He receives a text from Booboo once outside.

"Oh, oh. Mama, it's from Booboo."

"No need in not opening it. We have three blocks to walk back to the hospital. At least we had a good time."

"Ok, here goes. I'll look first. Oh, shit, mama."

"What happened?"

"Congratulations, you've just gone viral."

"I hate that camera crew. And I hate Arnez Harris even more."

DJ had a visit from the doctor early the next morning. He was awake and alert. All of his vitals read good, and he was hungry. Everyone was asleep, so DJ looked through his Cross'em Up Sports Magazine. His father slept in the room with him before, but never under the covers. Destin opened one eye and scanned over to DJ's bed.

"Morning little fella, did you have a long night? Why are you under the covers? Hey! You have a nightgown on. What happened?" asked DJ.

"I had a dog gon heart attack, son."

"I'm sorry, Dad. I know you were worried about me. As a family, we're in bad shape. The doctor told me that Mama fainted. Can you handle something else, Dad?"

"How much stuff can happen in one night?"

"We are *The Destin Family Reality Show*. We're always poppin'. Your ex-girlfriend has gone viral."

"Wow, look at Faye! Those Tae Bo classes are paying off. Her swing is incredible. She kept her left arm up, and looked at how she pivoted with her back foot. She caught him flush on the cheek with her right cross as he was moving away."

Destin's phone pinged with an incoming text message. "Hey, DJ. Listen to this. The lawsuit has been dropped against you. Our lawyer discovered that Mr. Melvin, the driver of the Jaguar that hit you, had been drinking and his passenger whom he was drinking with was underage. Mr. Melvin didn't want to explain why he was buying an underage girl alcohol in court. The bartender at the bar gave a written statement. And, now Mr. Melvin owes the truck driver for crossing into his lane and forcing the truck driver to hit him. You, my son, have been cited for reckless riding."

"If you're up to it, I want to tell you about The Dream."

"Booboo told me."

"Do you want to talk about it?"

"Yes, and no. I thought about how the media slandered his name and made him sound like America's most wanted. I have a story to tell of him that is different from when he took me on the road with him and you stayed home. He taught us the importance of praying before each performance and being allowed to perform in front of thousands of people shouldn't be taken for granted. He would say we are representing our culture and who we are as an individual. Don't embarrass ourselves. I loved him, Dad. Do you think his baby's mama shot him?"

"She testified to doing it. Turned herself in and gave a written statement. That's all we can go by, son."

Faye and Fatz showed up at the hospital, and DJ tried to get out of bed. Fatz quickly ran to his side and held him up. "Help me walk. I'm ready to get out of here," DJ admitted. The doctor was standing in the doorway. "Ok, let's take a walk."

DJ began taking steps like a baby with Fatz's help. All day long, he walked. When Fatz needed a break, Booboo filled in. The physical therapist massaged his body during the evenings, and in the morning, DJ was up and at it again. By the end of the week, he was doing squats and stretching. Fatz arrived early in the morning once DJ was fit to begin lifting weights. The doctor was concerned about his determination to recover and evaluated him every evening. His doctor was from Portugal and sometimes mixed languages when he spoke. He would apologize and continue. DJ understood every word he said. He listened to the doctor and one of the nurses talk in Portuguese by the side of his bed. DJ interrupted and began speaking in their language. His words were, 'I heard you say I should be able to go home within the next two weeks.'

Both the doctor and the nurse nodded their heads in agreement.

CHAPTER 14

THERE'S NO PLACE LIKE HOME

Destin had a meeting with Arnez Harris by Zoom because he wasn't allowed in the hospital.

"Mr. Harris, DJ will be going home in two weeks. We shot our last episode a week ago. Our contract with you has been fulfilled. I expect all of your equipment, and crew to be removed from my home before then. It has been a good eleven years, and it's time for us to part ways. I hope to keep a good working relationship with you."

"Is it more money you want? I can raise the pay of everyone."

"You can talk to everyone individually. But you won't be recording any more footage from my home. Understood?"

"Understood."

Each staff member who worked DJ's floor stood in a line to say their goodbyes to the family. The Destin Family had been there so long that they acquired a lot of things. They generously donated the items to the hospital. When first admitted, everyone who worked the floor had no idea who DJ was. All of them googled and watched his life on YouTube until they felt like they were his family. He received cards and small gifts, but no one wanted to see him go. Perks happened because DJ was there. For one, celebrities visited him once he came out of the coma. The staff had autographs from singers, actors, and athletes, along with photos. Hugs and tears filled the ward until the family were all gone.

Grace had formed a friendly relationship with every one of them. She knew all of their kids by name and met some of them. They opened up to Grace as if she was a therapist. Faye kept a mental note of all conversations and decided to bless all of them with gifts. The staff had no idea, and the gifts were delivered to their homes the day Destin's family left the hospital. One family member did not receive one hug or handshake from the staff. That would be Nancy. One after another, they said, "Bye, drama queen," and turned their backs to her and went back to work.

Destin knew he couldn't trust Arnez to remove all his equipment from the house. Before he brought DJ home, he had every piece of furniture removed. Everything inside the cabinets was removed and cleaned. He had the carpet removed, new tile laid, walls painted, and windows washed. Sixteen hidden cameras were found that were supposed to have been removed.

"Grace, baby, you did a wonderful job. I didn't know you had decorating skills."

"Are you thinking what I'm thinking?"

"Another business, venture?"

"Exactly, we have photos of the home before and after. I can post them and see what happens."

"Go for it."

DJ stepped into his newly redecorated bedroom and loved it. He lay across the bed and fell asleep instantly. Destin said, "Maybe we should have left one camera up. I've made a trip to his room six times to see if he's still breathing."

Grace and Destin have been living the life of a loving, mature couple. They traveled and created new ideas.

Faye had a new boyfriend named Dreymond, who continuously rang her bell. She wanted to introduce him to the family but dared not bring him to the big house after the last fiasco.

Fatz was about to open his luxury hotel and spent over $100 million to build it. Grace decorated every detail to perfection. Nancy lived in the Valley house without Fatz and the chef; they moved out altogether. The chef was now head chef of Fatz Cuisine, located in West Oakland. Fatz had his office and home on the top floor of the hotel. Nancy accepted the offer for her old job at $75,000 annually, a far cry from the healthy $200,000 she made before leaving. Nancy lived with Sheila during the week and drove home on the weekend. Sometimes she came along just to confirm some of these stories Nancy had been telling about the Destin Family.

Sheila couldn't get over the Valley house. Everything Nancy said was true. She asked, "Are you buying this from them? You can't afford this on your income. This is a beautiful house. Are you sure the chef is gone? Can I have a room here?"

"Yes, yes, and yes. Let's go visit my son. I want you to meet him."

The closer they came to the house, Sheila became nervous. "Nancy, where are we going again? This doesn't seem right."

"They stay up this street, and I have to make a right turn here. I am pulling into the driveway so don't freak out. I have the remote to open the gate. See, we are in. Girl, don't come in here acting as if you have not been anywhere. Sheila, stop crying. What's wrong?"

"This is beautiful. I'm so glad that you're my friend."

"Get your ass out of the car."

"They entered through the side door which led into the kitchen. It was quiet, no one seemed to be home. They heard footsteps, and Chip, the family dog, appeared. Sheila screamed. Nancy blurted, "Girl, I'm going to slap you if you don't pull yourself together. Let me call DJ and see where he is. I'm not walking through this big ass house." Chip sniffed Sheila while the phone was ringing. She was about to freak out until she felt his soft, silky coat and began to massage his head. He leaned up against her comfortably. "All the men in LA, and you hook up with a dog," laughed Nancy.

"Hey, Mama, I thought I heard voices. Who was that screaming?"

"This fool right here. This is my best friend, Sheila. The friend I stay with in Vegas."

"Nice to meet you, Sheila. I see you met Chip."

"DJ, can I see the rest of the house?

"Sure, Chip will show you around. You can see every room but my father's. It's ok. Chip is the tour guide. He knows the way. Good to see you, Mama."

"How do you feel, DJ?"

"Rested, bored. I was thinking about moving to Australia for a while. We are having a family meeting later tonight, so please stay."

"Baby, I'm here to see you. I'm not going anywhere."

Sheila had been gone for forty-five minutes when Nancy found her in the backyard deep in worship. "Hoe, what are you doing?"

"I'm praying for a house like this."

"Remember a house like this comes with a price. You sure you want to go through what they went through to have this house."

"Hmmm! Maybe I will shorten my prayer to a smaller house like this."

"Girl, bring your crazy self in here. Destin and Grace are home."

"Hey, everybody. We are waiting on Faye to log into Zoom and we can get this family meeting started, announced Destin.

"Hey, everybody!"

"Hi, Nancy."

"There's Faye. I don't have anything. We are scattered across the world now, and it's good to see your faces. Now, who has something to share?"

"I will go first," Raphael said. "DJ, there is a company that has made you an offer to buy Cross'em Sports; the offer is $1 billion. They think it's a fair offer. Are you interested in selling?"

"Did he say a billion?" asked Sheila.

"That is a nice offer. What are you thinking?" DJ questioned Raphael.

"Globally, your sales are up. Making the company worth at least $3 billion. They want to keep the name, meaning they want to finish the ride off of your success."

"For $3 billion, they can keep the name."

Sheila whispered, "Nancy, did they say $3 billion?"

"Yes."

Fatz said, "I have something. I have been thinking about this for a while. I need someone to run the Fatz Hotel in Oakland. I want to offer that job to Ms. Nancy, if she is interested."

Everyone in the family turned towards Nancy with surprised looks on their faces. Except for DJ, he already knew. Faye frowned up her face like a prune but held her peace.

"I'm offering this to you Ms. Nancy because I know you've been to school for this type of management position. In this short time I've known you, I've seen the professional and charm side of you. I've also seen your 'I don't play; you've picked the wrong one' side. And I think your balance is what I'm looking for. Besides all of that, you are family. You are my best friend's and brother's mother. I love him and I love you. I want to offer you this position before anyone else."

Nancy sat silently with her hands over her face. Her dream had finally come true. Her eyes cut over to Destin, full of tears.

"Take it," encouraged Faye. "He's right. You do deserve it."

DJ started to sing.

"The moment I wake up

Before I put on my makeup

I say a little prayer for you

While combing my hair now

And wondering what dress to wear now

I say a little prayer for you.

Forever and ever, you'll stay in my heart

And I will love you

Forever and ever, we never will part

Oh, how I love you

Together, forever, that's how it must be

To live without you

Would only mean heartbreak for me"

Everyone chimed in.

"I run for the bus, dear

While riding I think of us, dear

I say a little prayer for you

At work I just take the time

And all through my coffee break time

I say a little prayer for you"

Nancy took the lead.

"Forever and ever, you'll stay in my heart

And I will love you

Forever and ever we never will part

Oh, how I love you

Together, forever, that's how it must be

To live without you

Would only mean heartbreak for me

I say a little prayer for you

I say a little prayer for you"

"Yes, I will accept the job. Thank you Fatz."

"I have an announcement to make. Samantha and I are expecting a child," shared Raphael. Everyone was happy about the new addition to the family.

"That's not all," he added, "we are married." No one said anything for thirty seconds.

Nancy was the first to speak up, "Congratulations, Booboo!" This set off a chain reaction from everyone else but Grace, who was fuming. "Looks like our family is growing," Destin said with excitement.

"Raphael, call me now," Grace insisted.

"Looks like the family meeting is adjourned."

Nancy and Sheila took a week off and flew to Oakland with DJ to see Fatz's City. They began the tour inside Fatz Cuisine, his lavishly decorated upscale restaurant. Sheila pointed out several things that would minimize the traffic in high-traffic areas. In addition to that, she noticed a rather small space that could serve as an area for a sax player, a small band, or a comedian. They walked through the large entranceway that led into the waiting room. It was an extremely large space where only adults played interactive games while waiting for their tables. A circular bar area sat in the middle of the room. The loft was decorated with the artwork of local artists for purchase. Fatz held a raffle drawing every fifteen minutes to ensure that people waiting for their tables were always entertained.

The sports building was still in preparation mode when they entered it. "Supply chain backup was the reason that this project was not completed," explained Fatz.

Upon entering the Fatz Hotel, Nancy stepped back and admired his name on the building. "You have built up your name into a global company. I googled you. You have fast food restaurants in eight countries."

"This area will be the headquarters for all of my businesses. Let's start at the top and work our way down. My living quarters will be half of the top floor. The other half is my office and conference room. Everything you see here was picked out by Grace. The next two levels down will be the Presidential Suites. The rooms are smaller as we get to the first floor. I have this room set up for you if you need to stay overnight. And now let's talk about your pay. DJ shared your testimony with me. I am prepared to offer you the same salary you were making before you left Vegas to care for

DJ. I want you to be happy because you are going to have your hands full."

He continued, "Sheila, would you like the position of manager next door? All four places. I see you have an eye for improvement at no extra cost. That means a lot to me. I am preparing to offer you the same salary of $200,000 a year."

Nancy and Sheila hugged and laughed until their sides ached. They never knew that DJ would be the one paying their salaries. He invested the money so Fatz could offer the job to Nancy. Sheila was an afterthought, but DJ would pay her also. His generosity allowed Fatz to increase the hourly wage of the other workers. DJ was prepared to do whatever it took to make his mother happy.

They both ran their departments like drill sergeants when it came to time, dress code, cleanliness, and training. All disputes were taken to Nancy, and her decision was final. Sheila and Nancy played good cop and bad cop to negotiate a win-win for everyone. Nancy knew her position was offered because she was family. She maintained a positive attitude daily and passed it on to the staff.

During big events, they double-teamed to provide an excellent experience for the patrons dining or staying at the Fatz Hotel. Most nights, they stayed at the hotel because there was so much going on from day to day. They gave tours of the property and set up seminars and much more. Fatz offered one-week-long chef classes for thirty students during the week. The hotel was full of guests every month. Nancy and Sheila were known as "Double Trouble" around the Fatz Hotel.

Fatz Burgers tripled in income once he introduced the DJ Burger. He offered a $1,000 prize to anyone who could name the ingredients in the burger. DJ would make guest appearances to promote the burger, causing traffic jams for fans stopping by to see him.

CHAPTER 15

STILL IN LOVE

With a grandbaby on the way, Grace started making trips to Australia, trying to convince Raphael and Sam (Samantha) to move to

California. Raphael assured his mother they were not moving. To make sure she understood, they purchased a six-bedroom house in Sydney.

Once their baby girl Sammy was born, Grace moved in. Destin stayed for a while but always returned home. He had never spent time alone before now. Everything was taken care of, and all his family was living their dreams. Faye would come by and check on him occasionally.

"Hey Destin, I'm headed your way. Can I bring you anything?"

"A fat sack of cookies." The phrase was code to say Grace was not home.

Faye and Destin rekindled their relationship. She felt comfortable staying for the weekend without cameras recording their every move. They took in a movie or a play once a week, followed by an enjoyable dinner. Sometimes they would change it up and go bowling or skating at the beach. If Destin thought about Faye, she would show up with everything he needed, and when she left, Destin was good until her next visit. Faye had that Jill Scott look and build at 5'7", 165 pounds, a big-boned woman. She challenged Destin in the bedroom, and he worked hard to satisfy her. Faye moved around a lot when backing that thing up, forcing Destin to hold on to her handles or fall off. She would put that bear hug on him during her climax, which caused him to climax. And that caused a deep sleep to fall over the both of them. Faye no longer had to rush and leave, and Destin never wanted her to.

Grace was in Australia playing grandma. She was a beautiful woman by outward appearance; spiritually, mentally, and intellectually, she was complete also. Grace carried a small frame at 5'2" and 123 pounds. Most men could not dream of a more complete woman. In the bed, however, Faye ran circles around Grace. Most nights, Destin didn't work up a sweat with Grace. Before having sex with Faye, Destin would stage water and a towel by the bedside because Faye put the work in and had Destin weak in his knees afterward.

To Grace, it felt like she messed up during Raphael's early years and wanted to revisit those days with Sammy. Samantha was ready for Grace to go, but because of her love for Raphael, she never said a word. Instead, she learned to live with and learned from her. Samantha's mother had passed away when she was a child, and now she embraced Grace and the opportunity to have a mother-daughter relationship. Everyone in the Destin Family received what they wanted.

Destin left Los Angeles to visit The Fatz Hotel and spend quality time with DJ and Fatz. DJ had practically moved into the hotel. Destin enjoyed the atmosphere, and it felt just like the early days, except there was no stress on him. Grace and Raphael handled all the tax problems. The few rappers he signed were good guys and only came to him when they had business issues or needed help to broker a deal. Destin had Faye on stand-by if he needed a tune-up.

Nancy and Destin didn't talk much while he was there. He watched how Nancy and Sheila ran the business and was impressed. Sheila wanted to be part of the Destin Family and the reality show to be picked up again. Sheila was a few years younger than Nancy, but they got along like sisters. Nancy was the boss but consulted Sheila on most matters. She had more experience, and Nancy respected her knowledge and opinion. They never fought or argued. When they couldn't agree on a matter, they broke out a bottle of wine and talked it out.

Destin had no idea he walked up on a dispute. With his glass in hand, he said, "I like wine," and pulled up a chair. Both ladies looked at him and shook their heads.

"Private meeting, we are discussing business," responded Nancy.

Destin reached for the bottle of wine, "Cool, I'm great at discussing business matters." Sheila slapped his hand off of the bottle.

Nancy gave him the head nod to say, "Get on out of here." Destin took the hint and moved on feeling some kind of way. It was difficult to go from everyone calling your name and needing your advice to "Get on up out of here, we got this."

Destin called Grace and told her he was on the way. He lived at The Fatz Hotel for three months and was missing Grace. Once Destin arrived there, he noticed that the only person in the house who acknowledged his presence was Booboo. They worked out together every day because Booboo had become a bodybuilder. His whole day consistently included physical fitness, healthy eating, reading, and spending time with the baby. He embraced hot yoga one hour a day also. Destin started burning calories at a rapid pace. His cardiovascular boosted and improved his flexibility. His mind became free of stress when Raphael showed him the importance of meditation. Destin had gained a sense of peace and balanced it with emotional well-being. He followed Booboo's advice and gained 15 pounds of muscle in four months.

Back in Oakland, Destin had some pep in his step. His blood pressure and high cholesterol decreased, and he felt great. DJ saw him and almost went into a coma again. Destin stood tall, looked solid, and had lost his belly fat.

When he arrived at the hotel, there was a huge conference happening. The Women's Empowerment Conference was on its fourth and final day. Nancy and Sheila scurried around like chickens as they worked. Neither one of them knew Destin had returned. It was lunchtime, and both ladies had their shoes off. Sheila was rubbing her feet, and Nancy was massaging her neck. All of a sudden, Nancy felt a set of strong hands with long fingers take over rubbing the tension out. She never turned to see who it was; she took it all in, leaned her head back, and closed her eyes. Putting hands on Nancy's neck brought back memories of when she would come from the shower with only a towel wrapped around her body and lay across the bed. With her body still warm, Destin would take the oil, starting at the top of her neck, and massage his way down her long, defined body. His hands hugged her body like a roller coaster ride going around her curves. He stopped only to caress and kiss those places he knew she liked. By the time he would reach her feet, an erection was in the making. Nancy felt him against her back and turned to see who it was as if she didn't know his touch. It had been almost twenty years. Nancy stood up, pointed a finger at Destin, and walked away. He threw his hands in the air, sat in her chair, and drank out of her glass of wine.

Nancy walked by later and handed him a tightly folded pair of her panties. Destin opened his hands ever so slowly and discreetly brought them up to his nose for a sniff. Her aroma still tickled his nose after all these years. Nancy watched in amazement as a smile stretched across his face. "If you want it, you know what room I'm in," Nancy teased. Destin turned and walked away, scared to death. There was no turning back if he went to her room.

DJ wrote a rap honoring the legacy of The Dream. It played on different media outlets continuously throughout the world. DJ recorded it in four languages - Spanish, German, Tagalog, and French. Destin's phone was blowing up just like in the old days. He had no idea DJ made this rap song until Robby called him. "Let's take this show on the road. I know you've heard it by now." Destin turned on the radio, and it was playing. His son, DJ, who retired from rapping, had written another great Rap song of all time. In addition to that, he collaborated with the other artists signed to Destin to create a "We Are the World" type of song. With all the violence happening in the world, a sprinkle of love wouldn't hurt. Destin agreed, and the four groups went on an international tour.

The tour was successful, selling out stadiums and outdoor concert venues around the world. A full year of traveling was just what Destin needed. Not having to keep his eye on anyone and just enjoying the country brought Destin joy all over again. The last stop was Japan before they returned to the United States. DJ and Destin were out eating when a small Japanese girl, about five years old, walked up to DJ and pulled one of his braids. Destin snapped a photo of it for a keepsake. The little girl's name was Layla. She was Japanese and Black with beautiful brown skin, brown eyes, and a button nose. Her hair was long, black, wavy, and hung below her back. She climbed into DJ's lap at the table and began singing him a song while playing with one of his braids. Destin was concerned about this child's parents because no one had stepped up to claim this child. DJ said, "I'm going to take her home with me."

"Are you serious?"

"She has a beautiful voice. This could be a new venture for me. I'm no longer a rapper. I sold my motocross company. I have nothing to do but hang around The Fatz Hotel."

"I know that feeling. Let's see if we can find a parent."

A woman came into their view. "Hello I'm Lela, and that's my daughter Layla. Is she bothering you? She watches your videos all day and she can do all of your dances. She hugs the TV every time you're on."

"Come have a seat. This is my father Destin."

"I recognize him; you guys look just alike."

"Look who's talking," smiled Destin. Lela was beautiful. Also, a mix of Japanese and Black, she had the same skin color and hair with identical features to her daughter.

"Where's the father? If you don't mind me asking," DJ questioned.

"Military, overseas somewhere. He knows he has a daughter but doesn't want to be a family. I receive a check monthly."

"I'm going to remain here for a while and get to know you and Layla. I love her singing voice and want to sign her to my record label with your permission. How do you feel about that?"

"Let's ask her." Layla lay her head on his chest.

"I think that's a yes."

DJ asked Layla to sing a song that she knew. He videoed her from start to finish and posted it to TikTok. One hour, one million views. Destin commented, "I think you're on to something." When DJ found out that Layla could dance and sing, he posted another video. One hour later, one million views. Layla wanted DJ and Destin to come to her house to visit. As soon as they went through the door, Layla ran to her room and got her guitar, played, and sang a song by Prince. DJ asked, "What do I have to do to sign your daughter? I want to take you and her to the United States."

"We need to contact her father and get his permission to take her out of the country."

"Tell him he no longer has to pay child support and see if that helps." Lela sent the request, "Now we wait." A message came back in thirty seconds saying, "Send the paperwork." Destin got their Visas expedited, and they were on their way.

DJ had been creating a following for Layla, and now he was ready to write her a hit. Her followers were so widespread in age, that he didn't know what age group to go after.

Once they arrived in Los Angeles, DJ gave his 1,500-square-foot room to Lela and Layla, and he took Fatz's room. Destin asked, "You know what I'm thinking? A girls' group."

"That means babysitting. Who's going to do that?" They both turned and looked at Lela.

"Oh, hell no, gentlemen. You never said that was part of the deal."

Destin agreed, "It was just a thought." DJ decided to have Layla perform a remake of his mother's favorite song and send it to her as a special surprise. He thought to post it as a birthday gift and see how much attention it got. Little Layla laid into I Say a Little Prayer for You. She had no idea who Aretha Franklin was, but she sang her song with so much soul that Aretha would be proud. The next day was Nancy's birthday. At the hotel, Fatz was on stand-by to record her reaction. DJ sent the video, and Nancy went crazy. Fatz had it all on video. Within one hour, the video and reaction went viral. Over six million views and the video was shared for months. People began sending it to loved ones for birthday gifts, Get Well, I Love You, and Be Home Soon expressions. The video was better than sending a card. Nancy asked, "Who is that beautiful little girl? I want to meet her. She better not be your child, DJ."

"Do you want to meet her? I can make it happen."

"Bring her to me, son."

The next day, they were at The Fatz Hotel. Nancy lost her mind when she saw Layla in person. Half Black and Japanese. Her mama was half Black and Japanese also. Nancy joked, "What's going on here? DJ, this is your child. Why didn't you tell me?"

"Mama, this is Lela, the mother. I am not the father. Ask Dad, he was there when we met them."

"Well, welcome to the Destin Family. We just keep growing. I was thinking, if she's not afraid, we can showcase Layla in the restaurant tonight."

Little Layla not only sang at the restaurant, but she also sang on every network TV show. Every morning show and late-night show, her face was everywhere. Lela told DJ, "My baby needs to rest.

And now we have all these people following us and taking our picture."

"That's the price of being famous."

"You're not with us anymore for these appearances, and I'm scared someone will try to take her." Just then, Faye busted in the kitchen door with Chip. She kept the family dog while Destin was on the road.

DJ said, "Meet Chip. He is trained and won't let anyone near her while he is around. I will come with you guys to let Chip know what he's supposed to do. And you won't have any more trouble from the Hollywood weirdos." Layla and Chip got along instantly. They played all day until Lela laid her down for a nap, and Chip lay by her bedside. DJ stepped out for a while, and with the house quiet, Destin and Faye had some unfinished business to tend to. She hadn't seen Destin since he lost the belly fat and put on fifteen pounds of muscle. They went at it like a hurricane meeting a tornado for the first time. Lela was walking through the house and heard their sounds of lovemaking. She put her ear to the door because she thought DJ was in the room with a girl and got mad. Lela eased the door open, caught Destin on the down stroke, and closed the door quietly. Faye whispered, "Did you see that? Your door just moved."

"Faye, baby, I'm a hurricane. I make everything move." She raised an eyebrow and kept her eye on the door. Destin began blowing wind, so Faye whipped up a tornado on his ass.

Lela was embarrassed. She thought they left the house, and now she's seen Destin in all his glory.

On the next talk show that Layla appeared as a guest, Chip escorted her. Destin and Faye took Chip to the groomers beforehand and paid $600 for the complete service: a shave, bath, blow dry, nails clipped, and beard grooming. They were scheduled to be guests on *The People's Show*. Layla walked in with Chip by her side and introduced him. The host extended his hand to shake Layla's hand, but Chip blocked it. One of the staff took a photo and put on a t-shirt with the caption "Layla & Chip". One month later, a cartoon was created and called *Layla and Chip Adventures*.

Faye planned to visit The Fatz Hotel for a week and wanted Destin to come. He agreed, but he thought through each possible scenario concerning his situation. He was committed to one woman, and that was Grace. Faye knew, and she was cool with it. Nancy was on a whole other level. It had been almost twenty years since he did any gardening in her flower bed. He was glad that he walked away, not accepting her offer. Nancy and Sheila had both purchased their own homes and were dating off and on. Nancy got plenty of offers but refused to go out with anyone except to have a drink or dinner at the hotel. The smoother his game was, the less interest she had in him. Offers to take her places, gifts of diamond earrings, and bracelets did nothing for her. However, Sheila was a little different. She accepted all gifts and invitations for trips, concerts, plays, and sporting events. She was a few years younger than Nancy and was living the dream.

Clarence Dobb, better known as Clay, had been deployed to the Middle East for the last two years.

His unit returned to Germany, and he was happy to be home. Clay had extra money in his pockets and no longer owed child support. He could buy those 20s for his ride. Life was good until one of his buddies in the unit sent him a video of Layla singing. The message read: "Is this your daughter?" He opened Google and discovered that, in two years, his daughter had become an internet sensation. She had music videos, talk shows, her face on t-shirts, and a cartoon. "My baby is rich," Clay blurted out. He reached out to Lela. No answer and her number was no longer in service. Email, nothing. He reached out to her family and friends, but no response. Clay took to Instagram, TikTok, Facebook, and other social media networks. He posted a video saying his daughter was kidnapped, and he wanted her back. Gossip, gossip, gossip, all over the internet. Clay had created a following of five million and was gaining support. Word was out that DJ had kidnapped his daughter and exploited her for money.

Destin received calls from all over the world. Record executives were furious with him and DJ.

They promised to cancel all his contracts, performances, and clothing lines; anything that had to do with Layla was finished.

DJ called Fatz and Raphael, "Let's take a ride." The three of them walked into a popular military bar in Germany. Fatz knew about this place because he opened a Fatz Burger a mile from there. Clay sat with twelve soldiers from his unit and another twenty guys from the base. Fatz walked in and everyone put a smile on their face. He spent many a day in this bar and knew the owner and staff well. Raphael walked in, looking like a soldier. He was now 6'2" with broad shoulders, a body chiseled, and more fit than anyone in the bar. But no one knew who he was, and that's just the way he liked it. DJ walked in last, and everyone in the bar freaked out. The women and men couldn't believe it was him. They've seen him in all the old TikTok dance and motocross videos, the motorcycle accident that put him in a coma, and *The Destin Family Reality Show*. Everyone pulled out their phones and took selfies with the three of them in the background.

DJ approached Clay and asked if they could go somewhere to talk in private. Clay tried to flex, "If you have something to say to me, you can say it right here in front of everybody."

Fatz yelled, "If anyone leaves right now and goes to Fatz Burger, I will take care of the bill." The bar emptied in thirty seconds.

"You just took all my customers," the owner said.

"I will take care of you," promised Fatz. The owner knew Fatz would make good on his promise.

DJ started their conversation. "I am prepared to offer you a large sum of money to take down your post, and stop telling lies on social media."

"What sum did you have in mind?"

"Half a million."

"Not enough for exploiting my baby girl. I want five million." Raphael reached into his briefcase, pulled out some documents, and laid them on the table.

"What's this shit?"

"Documents, signed by you, agreeing to give up all paternal rights, to drop child support payments to Lela for Layla. This has been done legally. This is your signature, and we are prepared to sue you for slander," said Raphael firmly.

The bartender mumbled under his breath, "Take the half-million fool." Clay sat at the table with his arms crossed, not saying a word.

Fatz asked, "You want to make this difficult?" He called his commanding officer, handed Clay the phone, and the officer got in his ass. Fatz already told him the situation and what they thought was a fair offer to make this go away. When Clay handed Fatz back his phone, he agreed to take the half million, remove all the posts, and never mention this again.

Faye and Fatz strolled arm and arm around the facility like a high school couple at the prom. He showed off some of the new improvements and told his mother what he planned for the future.

Destin relaxed in the lobby, reading text messages on his phone. Nancy walked by, and their eyes connected. He looked around for Faye and followed Nancy to her room. She was on the clock but had a hot flash when she saw Destin. Nancy wrapped her arms around his neck and pulled him in close. He circled his arms around her waist, and their lips met. Nancy's juicy tongue filled his mouth. He raised her skirt and held her well-rounded butt. In her mind, it had been over twenty-five years since she held this man. This is my son's father and the fourth man I've ever been with. This is my ex-boyfriend. Nancy began unzipping his pants when they heard a knock at the door. They both froze in position. "Are you going to answer it?" whispered Destin.

"No, be quiet." Another knock, and they heard a voice, "Ms. Nancy, Sheila needs you at Fatz Burger. Are you in there?"

"I will be right there. Thank you, Frances."

"Some other time," Destin said quietly. Nancy fixed her clothes and face and wiped the lipstick off her chin and cheek. She turned to Destin and did the same. Nancy peeked out the door and sent

Destin out first. He looked to his left and walked down the hall to the right. Nancy left her room, looked to her right, and walked down the hallway to the left.

Nancy walked across the parking lot to Fatz Burger. She saw two school buses and knew right away this could become a serious situation if these were high school kids. She stepped inside, and it was the boys' and girls' high school soccer teams. Sheila was holding it down because this was nothing new for her. With the help of Nancy controlling the crowd, getting everyone seated first, and then taking their order, it worked like a charm every time. She was normally loud and assertive. You dare not disobey her. Sheila and Nancy both had a reputation at Fatz Burger for being the two women you didn't want to mess with. This group of students came regularly and knew the process. Sheila watched as Nancy worked her magic when she noticed a smile on her face the whole time and held conversations with the kids. She even posed for pictures, which was rare. Nancy only posed with celebrities. Sheila walked over, "What's going on? You're in a good mood for an afternoon. Did you get some?" Nancy stood with a smile on her face. She began breathing fast, panting and fanned herself, then shook her head. At that moment, Destin walked through the door. Sheila cut her eyes to see what made Nancy smile. Sheila smiled, "I want details," and walked away.

CHAPTER 16

DESTIN FAMILY ADDITION

Lela woke up on Saturday morning with just a sheet covering her half-naked body. She walked into her daughter's room to see if she was still sleeping. Layla was not there, and her eyes shifted to the clock that read 11 a.m. Lela walked over to the sliding glass door, peered out of the curtains, and saw her in the pool with DJ and Chip. The night before, Lela had been invited to a movie premiere by a rapper named Sugar Daddy and didn't get home until 4 a.m. She always drove herself to small events; when invited to a major event, she would hire a driver for the evening. But no one ever came by the house to pick her up last evening.

Sugar Daddy was handsome, funny, popular, and smart. Lela met him when she was out with a singer and didn't like how the evening was going. So, she separated herself from him, and that's when she met Sugar Daddy. He lived up to his name, always offering gifts and trips. Lela didn't think he was an honest man and chose not to trust him. All of her dates knew her through DJ. If he wasn't around, they would make a pass at Lela. They did not know that Lela could freely see whomever she wanted because DJ was not her man, but she wished he was. DJ gained Lela's respect because he never lied to her. She didn't have to sleep with him to get anything. Lela had

$128 million in the bank, drove the latest model Maserati, and dressed herself and Layla in the finest clothes. They stayed for free at the Destin Family house, where the famous reality show was filmed. DJ made her dream come true by helping her start a children's clothing line with one of the most famous children in the world wearing her line of clothing, her daughter Layla. Also, supported by Samantha, her three children wore Lela children's clothes on runways worldwide.

When Lela dated men, she would look up their approximate net worth, and compare theirs to DJ and her own. There was nothing most men could offer that she couldn't buy herself or take her anywhere she had not been nor get her into any place. A call from Destin or DJ provided Lela entry into any establishment in the world. Her only dream now was for DJ to love her.

Lela would plan events and invite DJ to come. Sometimes, he would show up alone, and Lela presented herself as the perfect catch in hopes that DJ would notice. Other times, he would bring a date to her disappointment. Lela would never say a word but treated the woman with respect. DJ noticed but never said a word either.

A big event was scheduled, and DJ had to be there with Layla to speak about how they met and her career going forward. The interview was the next day at the Mall of America. They arrived late at the hotel in Minnesota due to a delayed flight caused by heavy snowing all day. Once Lela made sure Layla was down for the night, she slid under the covers with DJ. Their sleeping arrangement was not uncommon when Layla was a little girl. She would sleep in between DJ and her mother all the time on the road. But Layla was ten years old now and sleeping in her bed. Lela wanted to warm her body up next to DJ's. They cuddled, spooned, and fell asleep. The next morning, DJ rolled over onto Lela; she parted ways to allow him an easy entry. She wrapped one arm around his neck and placed her other hand in his. This would be their first sexual encounter. Many men tried to sleep with Lela, but her mind was made up from day one. It would be DJ or celibacy. She did not want the reputation of being an easy lay and passed around from man to man. DJ had his eye on her for a while as he was familiar with the way this game was played and had not planned to give in easily. He loved Layla from day one, and that would never change. Lela carried herself as wife material, and DJ was ready to submit himself to her.

Both of them were hot and bothered in the right atmosphere. It was about to go down just how Lela had dreamed it. Freezing cold outside in Minnesota and steamy and sweaty inside.

"Good morning!" Layla cheerfully walked into the room.

"Layla, you know better. Knock before entering a room."

"Yes, Mommy. Can we call room service for breakfast?"

Before breakfast, DJ planned to propose to Lela. The ring was placed around her toothbrush. Lela talked to Layla while putting the toothpaste on the brush but never looked at it. She kept her talking because she was recording a video. Lela ran Layla out of the bathroom so she could brush her teeth. Layla backed out the door but kept the camera rolling. Lela put the toothbrush to her mouth, and the ring slid and hit her finger. She looked in the mirror, saw the ice sparkling at her, and screamed. Lela was overwhelmed and never saw it coming. Her legs gave way, and she hit the floor. Layla, still recording, screamed and dropped the phone to get DJ. DJ left the suite for only one minute when he heard Layla screaming his name down the hallway of the hotel. Everyone on the floor stuck their head out when they heard Layla scream. DJ ran back into the room to see Lela lying on the floor with blood streaming down her forehead.

DJ called 911, and within seconds, the hotel was a madhouse. News reports televised that a well-known rapper beat up his girlfriend in a hotel suite in Minnesota. DJ's photo was on every television station across the world. Destin was in Oakland having coffee with Faye and Nancy when the news coverage broke. An ambulance responded to a call from The Fatz Hotel because three people were experiencing heart attack-like symptoms.

The police interviewed DJ for only 5 minutes. Layla showed them the video, and they uncuffed DJ and let him go. Their mere words were, "Sorry for the inconvenience." Lela was patched up and refused to go to the hospital. She had no idea why she passed out until DJ showed her the video, and she screamed all over again. The EMTs and the police rushed back into the room.

Fatz had to care for three of the most important people in his life. He knew the story got twisted and didn't have to say it. He said to Destin, "Pop you should know better."

"They caught me by surprise with that one, son. My coffee went down the wrong pipe."

"Mama, you know the game. Why would you let your guard down?"

"No, son, I was having trouble breathing because I saw Destin over here choking half to death and I was scared for him."

"Ok, Ms. Nancy. It's your turn. Are you ok?"

"Is this the kind of lives you all have been living? I feel like I'm still having a heart attack.

Someone please, get DJ on the phone. I know my blood pressure is high and it's breakfast time."

DJ was on the phone with Raphael, telling him how he proposed to Lela. Raphael had no idea that his brother was all over the news for beating up his girlfriend. He laughed as DJ told him the story. DJ sent the video of Lela and a video of the police placing him in handcuffs.

"How is Lela?" DJ turned the phone around and let Raphael see Lela lying on the bed face down.

"Is she dead?"

"No, I showed her the video of her passing out because when she came out of it, she didn't know what happened. Now she's passed out again after seeing her rock glimmering in the mirror. I'm having second thoughts." Lela, lying across the bed, sat straight up when she heard DJ's statement.

"I'm good. My head just hurts a little. Yes, I will marry you."

"Did you hear that, Raphael? It's official."

"That's good news, my brother. Hey, why don't you have the ceremony here in Australia? I will take care of everything."

"How can I refuse?

"This is breaking news of the startling video of the rapper, DJ, accused of beating up his girlfriend in a Minnesota hotel. We interviewed Agnus Wheeler from Detroit. Her room was next door, and this is what she said. 'I heard screaming and yelling at about 5 a.m. this morning. I was terrified when I found out he had beaten her.'"

"And this is Gabe Porter from Kansas, sharing what he heard. 'I heard a young lady screaming for her life. My room is across the hall. I banged on their room door but he wouldn't answer. The coward!'"

"Standing next to me is Alicia, whose room was next door. 'I heard a door close, and five minutes later, I heard a little girl say, 'Daddy, Mama has passed out.' I opened the door to see him running back into the room.'"

Here's footage just released by TMZ showing that DJ was never in the room when the alleged beating happened. It was a slip and fall that caused damage to the young lady's head. The ex-rapper lost several endorsements, totaling a billion dollars. One day later, all endorsements were restored. No one could be reached for comments. Reporting live, this is Philip Wilkens from KRIT News in Minnesota."

"Guest list, flowers, ice sculptures, limousines, photographer, food, cake, liquor, disc jockey/MC, cooks, servers, band, venue, invitations, hotel reservations, wedding rehearsal, wedding dress, tuxedo, wedding colors, flower girls, ring bearer, bride's maids, groomsmen, minister, bride, and groom." Samantha asked, "Did I miss anything?"

"I think you covered everything. Remember all of this is a surprise, DJ is the only one who knows. Did you hear what I said, Mama? If Dad calls, you can't mention anything about the wedding being here. Everyone has been told it will be in a secret location. If you slip up and tell Dad, you've just told the world. He can't hold water. Samantha and I are handling everything. This is our gift to them." Raphael hoped his mother would keep quiet.

"I'm glad we had a nice, and simple wedding. I'm beginning to feel stressed writing out their to-do list."

"We have a lot of calls to make and places to go, and people to see."

"Call me if you need me," Grace reminded them.

DJ, Lela, and Layla arrived at Fatz City as it was now called. Everyone was excited to see the new addition to the family. Although they already knew and loved them, taking it one step further brought everyone closer.

Lela still had a small knot on her head from the fall. That was the first thing everyone looked at after hugging her. She covered it with hair the best she could. Nancy pampered Lela like she was a newborn baby. She wanted to know everything about her life and how many more grandchildren she could expect. Layla spent most of the day with

Destin and Faye. DJ hung out with Fatz, sitting in on meetings and making business deals.

Several businesses wanted to build a facility on Fatz's thirteen acres. Although the location was in one of the worst parts of Oakland, investors now lined up to make offers. One parcel of land selling price would cover the total cost of what he paid for the entire thirteen acres. If he sold two parcels, it would cover the price of the businesses that operate in Fatz City. Fatz was ballin' out of control. All of his business deals were a gold mine.

As Fatz and DJ rode around the city of Oakland, they decided to ride through DJ's old neighborhood. They rode MacArthur to 90th, across Bancroft to East 14th, and across East 14th to Avenue B. The old neighborhood had changed, but not for the best. They drove up to Sequoyah in the Oakland Hills, where they first met. The neighborhood looked good, with clean streets and freshly painted houses with manicured lawns. Headed back to West Oakland, they drove to Foothill Boulevard, turned left, and went by the Oakland Auditorium. Then they drove a lap around

Lake Merritt, headed to 7th Street, and parked in Fatz City.

On the ride back, DJ told Fatz where the wedding would take place. He knew the secret would be safe with him.

"That's a great location. Who thought of that?"

"Raphael's idea."

"Does Lela know?"

"Oh yeah, she loves the idea that all she has to do is show up. Most women would need to have their hands in it from start to finish."

"My brother, I think you've found a good one," smiled Fatz.

Nancy clocked out for the day and put the work burden on Sheila. She took Lela to lunch in Downtown Oakland to have some girl talk. Nancy asked about her parents, and Lela gave their background.

"My father is Jamaican, he lived in the Bronx growing up. Joined the Navy right out of high school. He spent time in Japan for many years and learned to speak the language fluently. He met my mom in the local grocery store outside of the military base in Okinawa. She worked in their produce department. My father charmed her with his ability to speak Japanese. They married six months later. We traveled the world with him for several years, and then my mom wanted to move back to Japan. She didn't like the world once she saw it. My mom needed to be stable, so my father brought us back to Japan and bought a house. My mom does a lot of gardening, growing various vegetables. We spent a lot of time together before I met Layla's father. I thought he would be the same kind of man my father was. But he wanted a trophy girlfriend, and once I became pregnant, he lost interest."

Lela continued, "My father passed away two years after Layla was born, and that sent my mother into a deep depression. Instead of working in her garden, my mother would sit in a chair outside and watch me tend the vegetables. We lost her one year later. It's been me and Layla alone ever since.

Nancy hugged her daughter-in-law-to-be and smiled, "You're marrying into a big family now. You will never be alone again. I guess you know DJ has three mothers in his life. I'm the biological mother, but he has two more women who helped raise him in my absence. Don't be surprised if you have to have this conversation two more times.

Samantha and Raphael lined up four hotels of interest. She asked, "How many people are on the guest list?"

"I forgot to ask. Let me call."

"Hey, Raphael. What's up?" DJ answered.

"How many people are on your guest list?"

"I plan to keep it small maybe 50. Do you need their names?"

"Nope, I will be in touch. Baby, only 50 people. This is going to be easy."

They chose a five-star hotel located in Sydney, Australia. Samantha's father is good friends with the owner and gets a discount on rooms, restaurants, and servers.

Raphael knew of a limousine company that hired him to correct their tax problems. They were happy to help out and offered six limousines to transport guests to and from any location while they were in Australia at a discounted rate.

Samantha knew several photographers from her years in the modeling business. She sent an email out to all of them, and they responded with their prices, deals, and discounts.

"Cake. Let's go cake shopping today," said Raphael. They looked at ninety different styles of cake online when Samantha suggested, "We need to narrow this down. I'm calling Lela. She wants a three-tier strawberry shortcake."

Samantha set up appointments at six different bakeries to taste their strawberry shortcake and see their three-tier wedding cakes. By the end of the day, they both disliked strawberry shortcakes, and Samantha finally picked out one decorated beautifully with whipped cream instead of frosting.

"Next on the list is an MC. We have to use Robby. I don't have to ask that one." Raphael knew he wouldn't need DJ's approval.

"Flower girls. We will be using our two little ones and Layla," smiled Samantha.

"Let's add Nancy to the list of flower girls. DJ said she wants to be in the wedding, and that's the easiest place to slide her in without any drama."

"Black and Gold are their colors."

"Did you say black and gold, for a wedding?"

"I'm the messenger, baby. Black and gold."

"We need a minister."

"DJ mentioned a rapper buddy of his that has given his life to Christ."

"You know he has to be an ordained minister, certified. We want this to be a legal marriage."

Faye stopped by Destin's family home and let herself in. She had several items in a bag for him. Lela was sitting at the kitchen counter in the middle of the day with her pajamas on but asked if she needed help bringing in more bags. Faye declined and asked if they could have a woman-to-woman talk. Lela knew it was coming and offered tea or coffee. The two ladies sat across from each other at the kitchen counter, and Faye began the line of questioning.

"Lela, how do you know you're ready for such a huge responsibility as marriage?"

"DJ prepared me."

"Sweetie I wasn't expecting that for an answer. Do tell!"

"Let me explain. I spent time with DJ for several months in Japan, watching and listening to his conversations. He helped me understand the way business works, and that all agreements don't work out the way they're planned. He showed me how to stand up for what I believe in, and walk away from a deal if it was not a right fit for me."

"Sweetie, I'm asking about marriage, not business."

"I'm getting to that part, Ms. Faye. I took those principles to heart, and as I began dating, I listened to what men were offering me and most of it was lies. Sounded good but something did not add up. Everything DJ offered me added up, and we benefitted from the deals he made on behalf of myself and Layla. He never lied to us. He was honest and sincere. My role is to give him the same things he gave me. I trust him with my life and he knows that. I want him to trust me with his life, and I won't stop loving him until the day I die."

"Ok, Lela, you sound like me when I speak about Destin. I believe you will be a great asset to this family. Welcome!

"How many more things are on the list, Sam?"

"Several more. We should complete the list in about four days." Raphael and Sam hadn't spent this much time away from home since before they had kids. Both of them were experiencing a newfound love for each other. As they walked together, they held hands, and star gazed into each other's eyes as if they'd never noticed the color. They sat next to one another when seated during lunch, and their noses touched as they talked. The two of them never squabbled when choosing decorations, colors, food, or music selection for the ceremony. When Raphael and Sam reported their decisions to DJ and Lela, a few changes had to be made, but no big deal for them. The thought of spending time together without the kids was glorious. For a few nights, they stayed out late and visited a comedy club and a "Paint and Sip" spot in downtown Sydney. Grace didn't mind at all. Being a grandmother was the greatest feeling in the world for her. With each day that passed, Grace took on more responsibility with the kids. Sam appreciated her because now she could plan all-day events with Raphael or spend much-needed time with old girlfriends from the modeling agency. She welcomed her leisure life back because of the gift from Grace.

As she sat in the hotel lobby alone, Nancy was sipping a cup of hot tea. A white male, with bronze skin, 6'4", salt and pepper hair, and beard, great posture, and beautiful blue eyes walked by Nancy. She dropped her napkin on the floor, and he knelt at the same time Nancy reached for it. The top of their heads touch. Nancy said, "That's a greeting I've never experienced before." He smiled and handed her the napkin.

"Hi, my name is Horace. Horace Golden."

"Hi, I'm Nancy."

"Nancy, are you related to anyone at the wedding?"

"Yes, my son, DJ, is the one getting married. I'm waiting my turn to walk down the aisle. I'm a flower girl."

"I thought you were going to say waiting to walk down the aisle as man and wife."

"One day I hope." Nancy smiled and patted the empty seat next to her. Horace talked with Nancy until it was her turn to walk down the aisle.

Rehearsal was long and boring, and Nancy was hungry and anxious to get back to Horace.

The wedding day came, and Raphael was receiving phone calls at 5 a.m. from people saying they were in town and wanted to attend the wedding. He had made plans to accommodate twenty extra guests with room and food. The closer the time got to the ceremony, the more people contacted him. Raphael asked Sam, "Did you give my number out? I'm receiving calls from people that are in town from everywhere."

"The only person I can think of who would do something like that is reality show host, Arnez Harris."

Raphael called him immediately.

"Hey, Raphael, what can I do for you?"

"Are you sending people to DJ's wedding?"

"You had a small guest list and I thought I would let people close to the family know what was going on. I did not send them. I bet they gave some nice gifts."

"Oh, my God! You're here, aren't you?"

"Sitting right behind Destin."

Raphael hung up the phone, walked inside the ballroom, and saw Arnez sitting three rows behind his dad. Raphael walked over to let him know that Mr. Harris had lost his ever-loving mind. Destin responded, "If they came all this way, let them in. I know he is planning to film this, so before his crew sets up, he is going to have to pay a pretty price."

"And he will pay," Raphael said.

Everyone was seated, and out walked DJ, Fatz, and two of his motocross crew, wearing black tuxedos with gold vests. The flower girls followed next. Raphael's two daughters came down the aisle, sprinkling the floor with flowers, dressed in gold-colored dresses. The guests all smiled, took photos and videos of the little girls, and commented on how beautiful they looked. One was three, and the other was five. Next was Layla and more "oohs" and "awws" sounded from the guests. Nancy walked in, the last flower girl, wearing a silk black dress clinging to every curve of her body. Her back was out, and glitter sparkled down the small of her back. Nancy was a brick house with a few different numbers, 34-22-38. On the hunt for a man, she didn't mind giving them a close-up look at the goods. The guest went from saying, "AWW!" to "DAMN!" There was a lot of whispering from guests asking each other, "Is that DJ's mom? Destin let that getaway? She must be crazy."

Another guest said, "I heard she went and got herself a white man. That's what I'm talking about."

"Can't no white man handle all that goodness? And I ought to know, I'm a white man," replied another.

Nancy walked to the front, sat her basket down, and waited for the ring bearer. Raphael and Sam's youngest child, who was two, didn't fully understand what to do. Nancy was to encourage him to walk towards her. Halfway down the aisle, the thought of laying in the flower petals overwhelmed him, and he sat down, fell back, and made a butterfly with the petals. Nancy sashayed down the aisle to assist, caught the eye of Horace, and winked at him.

Everyone stood to see Lela standing at the entrance in a designer black silk dress, tapered at the calf with an 18-foot gold train. With a black veil pulled over her face, she looked dangerous. Guests clapped and whistled until she reached the DJ's arm. Destin handed her over and took his seat in the front row.

Their vows were said quickly for a Hollywood couple's wedding. But they both wanted to keep it simple. The minister asked if anyone wanted to contest the marriage, and Fatz broke formation and mean-mugged the guests. No one said a word. The veil was lifted and DJ kissed his bride.

During the reception, many speeches congratulated and expressed well-wishes to the newlyweds. Fatz started it off, but couldn't finish.

His childhood friend and little brother had grown up and gotten married. It wasn't until that moment that he realized how God brought two kids together and gave him a real father to look up to. The speech ended when his voice began to crack. When a 6'4", 275-pound man's voice cracks, his speech has ended, and no one in the room better not crack a smile.

Nancy watched Destin, Faye, and Grace huddled up together and decided to crash their little party.

"You all look very happy," grinned Nancy.

"We are, I am so happy for DJ. He's been through a lot," Destin replied.

"When are you going to tell Grace you're fucking Faye?"

Faye growled, "You sorry bitch."

She came with the Tae Bo right cross aimed at Nancy's nose. Destin reacted quickly, snatched her hand down, and held it. Nancy threw her drink down and bawled up her fist. Grace grabbed her around the waist and swung her around, "Walk with me. Don't ruin your son's wedding day with your foolishness."

Nancy shouted, "Hoe, I was looking out for you. She's fucking your man."

"You dumb bitch. I know she is. Look, Nancy, I developed a condition after I had Raphael to where I could not have anything inside of me larger than a finger, and not longer. That's why my husband left me. I could no longer offer him sex. Faye and I had a talk years ago about this arrangement. I love Destin, and she loves Destin. She takes care of his needs and I take care of everything else. Oh! Now, you want to cry? You owe Faye an apology. Let's go get you cleaned up; this is a special day, my love."

Horace walked towards them and asked, "What happened?" Nancy was broken and couldn't look at him. He wrapped his arms around her and told Grace to go back inside. Nancy wrapped her arms around his neck and hid her face against his neck. Horace tried talking to her, but as soon as he lifted her head, Nancy filled his mouth with her tongue. "Walk me to my room," she said. He walked her to the door and kissed her forehead. Nancy opened her room door and thanked Horace.

Nancy had this sexy look in her eyes, pulled Horace by his necktie into the room, and closed the door. He wanted Nancy from the second he laid eyes on her. No one would look for either of them until it was time for the Mother-Son dance.

They spent the next forty-five minutes working out Nancy's issues. Nancy felt great; she had been saving herself for the right time with the right man, and Horace delivered. Nancy had no more animosity toward anyone. She pulled herself together, put her clothes on, and brushed her hair back. She reapplied her lipstick, thanked Horace for the lift, and left the room to find Faye.

Nancy approached Faye slowly and wrapped her arms gently around her from behind. Destin stood a few steps away to let nature take its course.

"Faye, I don't expect you to ever forgive me for what I've done to you today. I was wrong, I embarrassed myself because I was jealous. I ask that you forgive me. You've been tolerant of me for years and I keep pulling the same bullshit. I realize that and now it's time for me to woman up and find my own man. May I hug you?"

Faye stared into Nancy's eyes for fifteen seconds. She slowly opened her arms, wrapped them around Nancy's waist, and replied, "You know I almost knocked your ass out." They hugged each other tightly. Destin came and wrapped his arms around the both of them. Grace, Fatz, DJ, Lela, Raphael, and Samantha all joined in for a group hug and a family photo.

DJ broke away from the group hug and grabbed the mic. "At this time, I would like to have my three mothers, Nancy, Faye, and Grace, take the stage." Nancy, the first one on stage, took the mic from DJ, hugged him tightly, and addressed the crowd with Faye and Grace on each side of her.

"This is a dedication to Destin that DJ asked us to do. Destin, we want to give your flowers while you can still smell them. This song, I've been told, is one of your favorites, *Imagination*, a song by Earth, Wind, and Fire."

"Magic mirror, come and search my heart

Can you tell me what you see?

There's a thousand voices whispering

Songs and you're the melody

So, I imagine my heart with you

See what imagination can do

It's not hard to conceive love's ecstasy

Imagining you and me

Many, many days our shadows passed

Seeing visions of a new

Bright horizon set the morning light

Ooh, and that morning lights you

So I imagine my heart with you

See what imagination can do

It's not hard to conceive love's ecstasy

Imagining you, imagining you

Imagining me

The beauty we both can see

Faye chimed in, "Fa, la, la, la, la. Fa, la, la, la, la. La, la, la, la."

Grace did also, "Fa, la, la, la, la. Fa, la, la, la, la. La, la, la, la."

You're the dream we prayed would come along

To make real our fantasy

Day and night, you live inside our hearts

You're the flame of love to me

So, we imagine our hearts with you

See what imagination will do

It's not hard to conceive love's ecstasy

Imagining you, imagining me

The beauty we both can see

It's funny what love can do.

All I can think about is you.

Ooh baby, Yeah

It's funny how I feel this way

I wonder if I love today.

It's funny what love can do

We find ourselves only thinking of you."

"We love you, Destin!" smiled each of the ladies. Destin was still on the dance floor stepping to the music, when he was joined by Nancy, Faye, and Grace. They stepped to the instrumental: step to the left, sidestep to the right, break it on down, and freestyle. The dedication sung by the three ladies was live and viewed by six million people with 70,000 comments and 54,000 shares. Although fifty guests received invitations, 150 attended the marriage celebration.

As the night came to an end, Destin looked across the table at Grace and Faye, who were talking amongst themselves about the wedding and all the unexpected guests. He loved both of his women, and they loved him. Destin looked at the people on the dance floor and saw his son DJ, his new wife, and his beautiful granddaughter dancing the night away. He grew from a young, talented, dare-devil little boy to a businessman, a mogul. Fatz stood not too far away entertaining two women, which was his normal and seemed to be having a good time. He got that from Destin. Fatz saw the game his pops was playing. Raphael and Samantha served as the hosts, and they had their hands full, providing food, drinks, and sleeping accommodations for all the extra people. His best friend from the hood, Robby, was doing his thing in the DJ booth. Robby had become one of the most sought-after MCs in the world and landed a permanent job at the Next Level Nightclub in Las Vegas. Destin loved him as a brother; Robby had been on this journey with him from the beginning.

Then there was Nancy, the young love of his life; she sat and talked with Sam's father, Horace

Golden. Nancy must have put it on him because from where Destin was sitting, his view of them looked like intimate. He observed eye gazing, smiling, and finger grabbing. Horace helped Nancy out of the chair and escorted her to the mic. Destin sat up straight; he knew this was going to be good. Horace, in front of family, friends, and strangers, asked Nancy Hussle to marry him. She clenched his hand tightly and looked directly at Destin. Once he heard the announcement, Destin held his head back and closed his eyes, pretending to be asleep. Nancy, with a look of disgust on her face, excitedly accepted Horace's proposal. Destin leaned back in the chair with his hands interlocked across his stomach and closed his eyes, only to be awakened by the voice of Grace in his ear. Saying, "Come on baby it's time to go Nancy has turned the wedding out.

THE END

Author's Thoughts:

"Hey. I need you two to wake up. No napping in the middle of the day. I said, get up. We are going to be late. Did you know that both of you talk in your, sleep? One of you is crying in his sleep, and the other one laughing. DJ, you were fighting somebody, and forget about being a Motocross champion. And what grown man has dreams of being a rapper? You know you told on yourself, Destin. I know about your two hoes, Faye and Grace. Don't let me catch you with them, it's gon be smoke in the hood if I do. DJ, don't bring that Fatz boy over here. We don't have enough food for him to come over and eat every day. I swear as soon as I get a chance, I'm out of here. I can do bad by myself. And who the hell is Booboo? DJ, you better not be using the bathroom on yourself, you're too old for that. You can't live in a dream Destin. You are a dreamer."

The paragraph above was supposed to be how the story ends. One of my friends said to me, "This is a good story, why does it have to be a dream? Why can't a black story have a happy ending."

That made sense to me so I changed the ending.